BLACK AND BROWN IN AMERICA

CRITICAL AMERICA
General Editors: Richard Delgado and Jean Stefancic

White by Law:
The Legal Construction of Race
IAN F. HANEY LÓPEZ

Cultivating Intelligence:
Power, Law, and the Politics of Teaching
LOUISE HARMON AND DEBORAH W. POST

Privilege Revealed:
How Invisible Preference Undermines America
STEPHANIE M. WILDMAN
WITH MARGALYNNE ARMSTRONG, ADRIENNE D. DAVIS, AND
TRINA GRILLO

Does the Law Morally Bind the Poor?
or What Good's the Constitution When You Can't Afford a Loaf of Bread?
R. GEORGE WRIGHT

Hybrid:
Bisexuals, Multiracials, and Other Misfits under American Law
RUTH COLKER

Critical Race Feminism:
A Reader
EDITED BY ADRIEN KATHERINE WING

Immigrants Out!
The New Nativism and the Anti-Immigrant Impulse in the United States
EDITED BY JUAN F. PEREA

Taxing America
EDITED BY KAREN B. BROWN AND MARY LOUISE FELLOWS

Notes of a Racial Caste Baby:
Color Blindness and the End of Affirmative Action
BRYAN K. FAIR

Please Don't Wish Me a Merry Christmas:
A Critical History of the Separation of Church and State
STEPHEN M. FELDMAN

To Be an American:
Cultural Pluralism and the Rhetoric of Assimilation
BILL ONG HING

Negrophobia and Reasonable Racism:
How America Taxes Its Black Citizens
JODY DAVID ARMOUR

Black and Brown in America:
The Case for Cooperation
BILL PIATT

■ BLACK AND BROWN IN ■ □ AMERICA

THE ■ CASE ■ FOR □ COOPERATION

BILL PIATT

With a Foreword by David Dinkins
Former Mayor of New York City

NEW YORK UNIVERSITY PRESS

New York and London

NEW YORK UNIVERSITY PRESS
New York and London

Library of Congress Catologing-in-Publication Data
Piatt, Bill.
Black and brown in America : the case for cooperation / Bill
Piatt.
p.   cm.—(Critical America)
Includes bibliographical references and index.
ISBN 0-8147-6645-5 (alk pap)
1. Afro-Americans—Relations with Hispanic Americans.   2. Hispanic
Americans—Social conditions.   3. Afro-Americans—Social conditions.
I. Title.   II. Series.
E185.615.P48   1997
305.868—dc21   96-45863
                          CIP

New York University Press books are printed on acid-free paper,
and their binding materials are chosen for strength and durability.

Manufactured in the United States of America

10   9   8   7   6   5   4   3   2   1

To Rosanne, Seana, Bob, and Alicia

and

to the memory of Haywood Burns

(1940–1996)

Contents

Acknowledgments xi
Foreword by David Dinkins xiii
Introduction 1

1 · The Way We Are 4

2 · How Did We Get Here? 13

3 · Who Are We Really? 24

4 · Jobs: Competing for a Shrinking Pie? 49

5 · Education: A Crumbling Commitment 67

6 · Language: Speaking to, and about,
One Another 91

7 · Gangs 109

8 · Voting: Coalition or Collision? 124

9 · Bringing Us Together 153

Notes 181
Bibliography 185
Index 193

Acknowledgments

I am very grateful to Leona Wyatt for typing this manuscript. I appreciate the assistance of the Texas Tech University School of Law students who helped me with research: James Abbott, Teresa Cardenas-Trowers, Amy Hale, and Pierre Woods. I am particularly grateful to Texas Tech students Andrew Tolbert and Michelle Kwon for their contributions to chapters 4 and 5, respectively.

Foreword

David Dinkins

This thoughtful, thorough, accessible work adds a great deal to the discourse on diversity and coalition-building in the contemporary social and political arena. The concise, insightful delineation of the very problem of categorizing minority group members opens the work effectively and appropriately. Dr. Piatt then goes on to discuss in lively and informative detail the relationships between African Americans and Latinos, and the case for cooperation over competition. He documents his work with statistics, but recognizes their limitations, and expands and enlivens his reasoning with humanizing accounts. He does an excellent job recounting the history of his subjects—including the shadows of the past—but he believes in the hope of the future, and calls for discussion, peacemaking, and cooperation. Dr. Piatt writes with clarity and respect for his subject, and this work is an important addition to the body of knowledge on racial and ethnic issues in America.

While we may have many pasts as Americans, we share one future as America. As I've said many times, your ancestors may have come to this country on the Mayflower or they might have been among those who welcomed that ship. Our ancestors may have come here seeking religious freedom, on ships that served as churches. Your ancestors might have come here on immigrants ships, fleeing persecution and seeking opportunity. Or they may have come whipped and chained in the holds of slave ships, as did mine. But irrespective of whether your ancestors were already here—and irrespective of the ships they came on—we're *all* in the same boat *now* and we *must* get along and make the most of it.

The central question of the American experience is *e pluribus unum*—how to make one out of many. The strength of our uniquely American alloy is tested often and rigorously throughout our nation, as hundreds of cultures seek to coexist. Our interactions reflect our different pasts and varying experiences, and, up to a point, that's a healthy thing. But we can sometimes get so caught up with what's behind us that we fail to look ahead.

Scholars tell us that problems arise when different social groups come into contact. It's an old story, one as old as our nation itself. In New York in the mid-nineteenth century, gangs of "native" New Yorkers attacked Irish immigrants right near City Hall, at Broadway and Park Row. Irish Americans lashed out at African Americans in the bloody Draft Riots of 1863, leaving many lynched in the North at the same time as our nation fought to free them from slavery in the South. In the 1870s, gangs rampaged against Italians and Jews. During the Depression, Jews were assaulted for advocating that our country intervene in Europe to fight the fascists and save the Jews. Today, different groups jostle against one another, and accuse each other of enjoying unfair advantages in the competition for scarce government resources. We all know our country's past failings—from its ill treatment of Native Americans and African Americans to its ill-advised adventure in Vietnam. But the history of America is still an open book—and, as Dr. Martin Luther King, Jr. noted, "The time is always ripe to do right."

As Dr. Piatt suggests, let us look not so much to our separate pasts as to our common future. Let us treat every day as a new opportunity to do right—*especially* for our children. It is for the sake of our children that the great multicultural experiment that began five hundred years ago must succeed. And with the help of Americans, assisted by honest, lucid discussions like that of Dr. Piatt, it *will* succeed.

We can all learn from this outstanding work.

BLACK AND BROWN IN AMERICA

Introduction

I shudder when I hear or read in the media that "Hispanics will soon become the largest minority group in this country." Why do we feel compelled to identify a largest, and implicitly most important, minority group? What will be the reaction of African Americans and Hispanics to these demographic realities? What has been the historical relationship between Blacks and Hispanics? Which interests of these groups coincide? Which collide? Who stands to gain or lose by African American and Hispanic cooperation or competition?

To the extent that there is such a thing as hard data, here it is. The United States Census Bureau projects that the Latino population in the United States will surpass that of African Americans sometime around the year 2005. By the year 2010, the Bureau projects that 203.4 million Whites, 40.5 million Hispanics, 37.9 million Blacks, 16.2 million Asians, and 2.3 million Native Americans will live in the

1

United States. This will result in a population that will be
67.7 percent White, 13.5 percent Hispanic, 12.6 percent
Black, 5.4 percent Asian, and 0.8 percent Native American.
By 2050, the population will be 52 percent White, 23 percent Hispanic, 15 percent Black, 10 percent Asian and 1
percent Native American.

Nonetheless, there are serious limitations upon the use
of even this apparently objective data. One limitation is
that the projections are only that. Second, the projections
are based upon the self-identification by human beings
within the supposed groups. As will be seen in this book,
this self-identification process is fluid. It depends upon a
relatively artificial categorization and pigeonholing process. For example, while there were certainly peoples of
Hispanic or Latino origin in this country prior to the 1950s,
one would not be able to confirm that fact by examining
the census figures. Indeed, until 1950, Hispanics were not
identified separately in the census. The changes in our self-
identification may reflect the realities that race may not
be an objectively identifiable nor even morally relevant
consideration.

The differences between African Americans and Hispanic Americans are not as pronounced as the pigeonholes
suggest. More and more Americans of color may begin to
self-identify as "multicultural," "multiethnic," "multiracial," or as some other category that has not yet been la-
beled. Just as many Hispanics now living cannot find themselves in the 1940 census, there are millions of Americans,
alive now, who will look back to the 1990s from some point

in the future, and not be able to find their multicultural, African Latin identity recognized. There are other limitations on the use of these numbers. Interracial marriages are growing in number. Immigration continues, as it always has, to redefine America. American society is moving toward a demographic mixture sometime after the year 2050 where Whites will hold a plurality but not a majority.

If I had to categorize myself, I would self-identify as a multicultural male. The Census Bureau doesn't allow that. If I can only select one box, it is "Hispanic." However, my background and interests are broader than any categories. The backgrounds and interests of the members of the groups that have inspired this work are also much broader than any categories. The challenge facing African Americans and Latinos, for their own prosperity and for that of America, will be to maximize the areas of mutual cooperation and minimize supposed, perceived, or even real differences. It is in this spirit that I offer this work.

1 ■ *The Way We Are*

We need to be blunt in approaching Black/Brown relations if we hope to improve them. Whether we want to admit it, in too many areas we may be at each others' throats. Yet despite the areas of conflict, we share a great deal of common concern. Both African Americans and Hispanics arrived in what is now the United States before Whites. Both groups have endured a legacy of bitter discrimination at the hands of Whites. Both groups are perceived to be not all that different by many Whites. As one Southern White explained, "Mexicans are niggers that don't talk plain."[1]

Perhaps because the media is quick to highlight areas of Black/Brown confrontation, the animosity between the two groups may be somewhat overblown. Yet it exists. It simmers in resentments and grudges, localized and not verbalized. Occasionally it explodes into violent confrontations.

I am indulging in overgeneralizations to make these initial points, but many Blacks feel that Hispanics are unfairly reaping the benefits of civil rights gains won by Blacks over centuries of struggle. On the other hand, many Hispanics feel their presence and needs have been overlooked in the Black struggle for civil rights. U.S. senator Joseph Montoya (D-N.M.) verbalized this concern in 1972:

> We are the "invisible minority." While the Black man has made the crying needs of his Ghetto children part of the nation's known history and collective conscience, we remain unseen. . . . Our efforts are fragmented. . . . And so in fragmented disorder we remain impotent; given hand-me-down programs; counted but not taken into account; seen with hindsight but not insight; asked but not listened to; a single brown face in a sea of black and white.[2]

Hispanics note with dismay that there never have been predominantly Hispanic institutions of higher education, nor has there ever been a Hispanic Justice of the Supreme Court of the United States.

Blacks fear being displaced by Hispanics in affirmative action programs. The media feeds this fear with a drumbeat of "Hispanics Soon to be Largest Minority" articles. Members of both groups, themselves the victims of White oppression, seek to vindicate themselves, or perhaps even subconsciously curry White favor by oppressing members of the other group. It is a vicious cycle.

Sometimes the conflict explodes in violence. Miami, for example, has witnessed a horrible series of conflicts between Blacks and Hispanics, resulting, in the 1980s, in four major race riots. Antagonistic relationships between disenfranchised Blacks and a more affluent Cuban American population is seen as the source of virtually every racial confrontation.

The political tension between these groups surfaced again in June 1990. Nelson Mandela visited Miami only to be snubbed by the administration of then Miami mayor, Xavier Suarez. Mayor Suarez and other Cuban-born officials indicated unease with Mandela's leftist leanings and his communist ties. The snub infuriated Black leaders in the Miami area who view Mandela as an icon in the worldwide struggle for Black liberation.

The tension between Blacks and Hispanics in Miami involves more than political feuding and differences. It has included bullets, rocks, and bottles. In 1989 a Hispanic Miami police officer, William Lozano, shot and killed two Black youths on a motorcycle. Rioting followed the shootings, just before the 1989 Super Bowl. Lozano was convicted, but his conviction was overturned by a Florida appeals court, which found that the threat of another riot in the event of an acquittal tainted the jury's deliberations and prevented Lozano from getting a fair trial. To the surprise of the media, no rioting broke out when the reversal was announced. Two days after the reversal was announced, however, another police shooting resulted in more rioting. On Thursday, June 27, 1991, a Miami police officer shot a Black man who the officer claimed aimed a gun at him. Some witnesses said that the man had thrown down his gun before he was shot. Black youths threw rocks and bottles, breaking windows in a city bus and in a police station, and numerous injuries were reported.

Los Angeles, too, has been the site of tremendous tension between Blacks and Hispanics. In Southgate, Hispanic parents objected to sending their children to a predominantly Black high school. In Compton, Black city officials objected to hiring more Latinos. In numerous schools in the Los Angeles area, groups of African American and Latino students fought each other repeatedly. The Martin Luther King, Jr./Drew Medical Center in Watts was the scene of intense confrontation between Black and Hispanic county employees over hiring and promotion. Violent confrontations occurred between Blacks and Hispanics at a detention facility in the Los Angeles area.

Following the Los Angeles riots, racial tensions escalated over employment opportunities. In July 1992, a Latino group described an incident in which they claimed Latino laborers were attacked and chased off a construction site by about thirty-five Black men who were objecting to the fact that no Blacks worked there. Racial divisions between Hispanics and Blacks proved to be a problem in other phases of the post-riot rebuilding efforts. Hispanic city councilors protested to Mayor Bradley the composition of the board of "Re-Build L.A.," the post-riot renewal group. The political conflicts drew upon the anger and resentment of some Hispanics who felt that Blacks, westside liberals, and a downtown business community constituted the core of the mayor's support and interest to the exclusion of Latinos.

Washington, D.C., has also witnessed strife between Blacks and Latinos. The increasing verbal tension erupted in physical violence on July 4, 1993. On the nation's birthday, in the nation's capital, Blacks and Latinos brawled in a predominantly Black area of D.C. Economic competition, immigration concerns, language issues, and a whole host of problems (discussed later in this book) seemed to spark the violence. On January 26, 1994, the owner of two Black-oriented radio stations in D.C., Kathy Hughes, complained that Hispanics have "taken over" parts of Washington, D.C. She also complained about overcrowded Hispanic apartments and Hispanic drunk drivers. This is not the first time that Hughes had angered the Hispanic population. After the 1991 disturbances in D.C.'s Mt. Pleasant section, Hughes noted that Mayor Sharon Pratt Kelly had restrained the police because the Mt. Pleasant section had a Hispanic population and "she was not on such good terms with Hispanics."[3] In a February 6, 1993, article in the *Washington Post* entitled "Treatment of D.C. Latinos Called Appalling by Panel," the authors discussed police abuse and denial of rights suffered by Latinos at the hands of Black officials. In a reversal of the Miami police shootings, the May 5, 1991, disturbances in the Mt. Pleasant area erupted after a Black police officer shot and critically injured a Hispanic man.

Variations on the theme of Black/Brown conflict have occurred throughout the country. In 1994, Latinos alleged that racist policies have kept Latinos numbers down at subsidized housing programs run by the city of Chicago, because Blacks were being given the opportunities. In New York, endless examples of cooperation and contention surfaced in recent mayoral elections. In virtually any urban area in the United States, confrontations between Blacks and Hispanics have occurred and continue to occur. Even smaller areas are not immune. In Lubbock, Texas, in 1995, two Hispanics and a White man were convicted of a federal "hate crime" offense after driving around the city shooting black men with a shotgun. The perpetrators announced they wanted to start a "race war." Not all confrontations rise to the level of a dramatic shooting or riot; most are played out in the schools, workplaces, prisons, and market-places.

Even where the confrontations do not rise to a visible level, the attitudes harbored by each group about the other reflect the potential for devastating conflict. In a recent poll of Hispanic residents of Los Angeles conducted by a Spanish-language television station, respondents were asked to identify the group that "Hispanics have most trouble with." Sixty-seven percent of the respondents said Blacks were that group, while only 14 percent identified Anglos.[4] A Louis Harris poll conducted in 1994 found many Blacks and Hispanics agreed with the negative stereotypes of each other. Forty-nine percent of Blacks said Hispanics "tend to have bigger families than they can support." Fifty-one percent of Hispanics agreed with the statement that Blacks "are more likely to commit crimes and violence."

Statements by civic leaders often add to the tensions. Jack Shakely, the president of the California Community Foundation, was quoted publicly as stating that "Latins are very, very prejudiced. The Latino is about as anti-Black as a Southern Baptist in Mississippi."[5] And, of course, in the private conversations of some Blacks and Latinos, there is the concern, sometimes expressed in an articulate fashion and sometimes with slurs, that the other group is being given unfair advantages and consists of basically unworthy human beings.

There are of course, people of goodwill on both sides of the equation struggling to help educate others regarding the need for cooperation. Every one of the instances of confrontation identified so far has been met with a series of public and private attempts at conciliation. Unfortunately, those in attendance are usually preaching to the converted. By definition, those individuals interested in furthering strife between races are unlikely to offer solutions toward improving race relations. Similarly, the conciliation meetings do not offer soundbites or video clips that are nearly as exciting or dramatic as a group of minority youths who throw rocks at one another or exchange gun fire. The mainstream media seem to have little concern for presenting the stories of successful peacemakers. (This phenomenon is not limited to race relations.)

Nonetheless, before spending more time dwelling on problems, it is important to note attempted solutions. In Washington, D.C., official and unofficial attempts have been made to calm tensions. Forums sponsored by civic organizations, government agencies, and religious groups have been moderately successful in setting a tone for dialogue rather than confrontation. Similar efforts have borne fruit in Dallas, Los Angeles, and New York. The private sector has been actively involved as well. In 1991, radio station KJLH in Los Angeles ran billboards featuring Muhammad Ali and Cesar Chavez gazing together at something in the distance with the caption, "We listen together, let's live together." Other radio stations in Los Angeles ran public service announcements encouraging racial harmony in the wake of the rioting following the acquittal of the Rodney King assailants. Throughout the country parents have contributed time and effort to peacemaking efforts following Black/Latino conflicts in the schools and in the streets.

Perhaps the most successful and clearly the most unnoticed efforts are those of individuals. At a mall, for example, a group of Hispanic youth gather to greet each other and hang out. A Black man walks by. One of the Hispanics, in a taunting voice, calls out, "There goes another 'mayate.' " The term is derogatory and is intended to insult the Black man. He pauses for a second, and looks toward the group. One of the other Hispanics turns to the first, and in a voice loud enough to be heard by the Black man says, "Shut up man, he's just like you and me." Tensions ease, and the man walks away. A Black woman, passed over for promotion by her Hispanic supervisor, challenges the determination but declines to make it a race issue. Hispanic workers, after having won a fight to speak Spanish on the job, voluntarily switch at some points in the conversation to English in order to include their Black co-worker in the conversation. Black and Hispanic civic, political, and educational leaders seek common ground to maintain affirmative action in hiring decisions, and consistent fair treatment for all applicants in matters of public assistance. Parents teach their children to be respectful of all members of society and to reject race-based characterizations and prejudice. These are not steps that will make the evening news; they are steps being taken to defuse what might otherwise continue to become explosive confrontations.

But no change in the hostile and antagonistic ways we often treat one another will occur until we acknowledge and identify the problems. The message is often painful. The messenger may not be welcomed. If not handled properly, the discussion can open old wounds and create new ones. It is time, if we are serious about addressing Black/ Brown issues, to learn how we got here.

2 ■ *How Did We Get Here?*

ispanics and Blacks arrived in what is now the United States well before non-Hispanic Europeans did. They have a long history of interaction in the western hemisphere. Like all other Americans, they are here as the result of migration, voluntary and otherwise.

Since the beginning of humankind, people have migrated in search of better living conditions. With the possible exception of a few linear descendants of the first humans who were born in Africa, virtually every human being in every country on the planet is a descendant of someone who moved or was moved to the area where he or she now lives. Even the people to whom we now refer as "Native Americans" were not native. Their ancestors entered what is now the North American continent over a land bridge from Asia somewhere between 40,000 B.C. and 60,000 B.C. By the time the Spaniards and Africans had arrived, the Native Americans had developed highly sophisticated governmental systems throughout what are now the Americas. Their achievements included well-developed trade and agriculture practices. The arts, sciences, and medicine flourished. By the time of Columbus's arrival, between 75 and 145 million "Native Americans" lived in the Americas. Somewhere between 7½ and 18 million of these people resided in what is now the United States and Canada. By comparison, Europe's population at this time was perhaps 60 to 70 million.

Columbus's arrival in 1492 eventually led to the exploration, in 1513, by Juan Ponce de Léon of what is now Florida, although a permanent Spanish colony was not established in that area until 1565. Meanwhile, Cuba had been colonized under the Spaniard Diego Velasquez in 1511. In 1519 an army led by Hernan Cortez left Cuba for the area which is now Mexico. A brutal military campaign resulted in the conquering of the natives and the establishment of Spanish colonial rule in Mexico. From that base, in turn, other Spanish "conquistadores" explored northward into what is now the American Southwest and Midwest. Cortez's conquering entourage included Africans, though it is not certain whether they were free or enslaved. The first record of African slaves in Mexico appeared in 1523. These Africans were brought for the purpose of providing household labor as well as to work in silver mines, the textile industry, fisheries, and in the growing and harvesting of sugar. By the time slavery was abolished in Mexico in 1829, approximately 200,000 slaves had been brought from Africa to Mexico.

Juan de Oñate established what has survived as the oldest continuous European settlement in the southwestern part of the United States at Gabriel de los Españolas, near the town of Española in northern New Mexico. Santa Fe was founded in 1609 and other settlements soon followed in what is now Colorado, Arizona, and Texas. Spain established these settlements with the religious and political goals of spreading the Spanish empire, its tongue and culture, and the Catholic religion.

Africans accompanied and participated in the exploration and settlement process. As historian David Weber has noted: "Despite the enduring myth that 'Spaniards' settled the border lands, it is quite clear that the majority of the pioneers were Mexicans of mixed blood. In New Spain, the three races of mankind, Caucasian, Mongol, and Negro, blended to form an infinite variety of blood strains, and this blending continued as Mexicans settled among aborigines in the Southwest. Thus 'Mestizaje' or racial mixture, was so common that today the vast majority of all Mexicans are of mixed blood."[1]

It is important to recognize that not only did Africans accompany the Spaniards to the New World, the Spaniards themselves carried African blood. A Muslim army from Africa invaded Spain across the Strait of Gibraltar in 711. By 719 Muslim power was supreme and the Spanish peninsula was held as a dependency of the province of North Africa, a division of the caliphate of Damascus. The caliphate eventually split into a number of independent and mutually hostile Moorish kingdoms. Subsequent Muslim sects from Africa invaded Spain in 1086 (Almoravids) and in

1145 (Almohads). Eventually, Christian kings expelled most of the Moors following a great battle fought on the plains of Toledo in 1212. However, the African Moors were not completely vanquished until 1492. Thus, for most of the seven centuries prior to Spain's arrival in the New World, Africans lived in and ruled Spain, and undoubtedly transmitted some of their blood to the Spanish conquistadores.

The Spaniards developed a nomenclature and a caste system in the New World depending upon place of birth and blood mixture. From the top of the structure reigned the Spaniards, also known as *gachupines* ("those who wear spurs") or as *peninsulares.* Next were the *criollos* (creoles), who were the white descendants of Europeans who had settled in America. The next class consisted of *mestizos,* those whose fathers were Europeans and mothers were natives, followed by *mulattoes,* those of mixed African and European percentage. Below them on the social rank were Africans, and last of all, natives. These categories were enforced by custom and by law. When only one-sixth of African or Indian blood ran in the veins of a colonist, she or he was by Spanish law given the designation *que se tenga por blanco* (white).

Creoles were generally raised in relative affluence. They were afforded privileged positions in the church, army, or the law. Because the mestizos had Spanish blood, they too were allowed a relatively favored life-style. Although often darker in skin color, mulattoes were seen as *gente de razon* ("people of reason") because of their white blood. Natives were generally regarded as the mental equivalent of children.

When the Portuguese settled Brazil they too created a caste system based on blood mixtures. In addition to categorizing mestizos and mulattoes, the Portuguese recognized a *sambo* as a person of mixed Negro and Indian blood. When a person carried mixed Portuguese, Native American, and African blood in unknown proportions, that person was referred to as a *meti*.

The Spaniards were the first but obviously not the only European colonizers in what is now the United States. Beginning with the settlement at Jamestown in 1607, the overwhelming majority of new arrivals to the areas that would become the American colonies were English-speaking Europeans. The result of this European immigration and subsequent conquest of the native populations was devastating. Europeans unleashed barbaric campaigns aimed at eliminating all native peoples. The horror of these campaigns included hanging and burning natives alive in groups of thirteen "in honor" of Christ and the twelve apostles, as was done by the Spanish. American soldiers slaughtered native women, cut off their genitals, and wore them on their hats.

Diseases carried into the New World were also devastating to the indigenous population. The net effect was the entire destruction of some Indian tribes and nations, a catastrophic population decline in the magnitude of 95 to 99 percent of native Americans, and a total death toll of perhaps as many as 100 million.[2]

Once much of the native population was destroyed or subdued, European colonialists established their own governmental and commercial systems. On the East Coast,

English colonies rebelled in 1776, and established the United States of America. From there, the country expanded westward and into the Southwest. While the first Blacks and Hispanics arrived voluntarily in what is now the United States, the growth of the colonies and the later expansion of the nation meant that Africans and Hispanics would be involuntarily incorporated. Africans were brought as slaves and Hispanics were made part of the country by a conquering military force.

The slave trade ended, by one conservative estimate, with at least 350,000 Africans entering the United States beginning in colonial Virginia in 1619. Many others were shipped to other parts of the New World, and still more died in the process of being captured and transported. The entire process resulted in the deaths of as many as 30 million Africans. Not all slaves remained slaves. Some escaped and fled north, where they were welcomed by various Native American tribes. United States soldiers who arrived in what is now the American West were amazed to find Black Indians—the offspring of these slaves and natives.

In 1836, Texas won its independence from Mexico following a war. In 1845, the United States annexed Texas. The boundaries, however, remained unclear. In 1846 a skirmish occurred between American and Mexican troops on the north bank of the Rio Grande, an area where both Mexico and the United States claimed sovereignty. President James Polk claimed that the United States had been invaded and obtained a congressional declaration of war. Many matters involving U.S.–Texas-Mexico relations, including the location of boundaries, interpretation of factual events, and even the factual events themselves continue to be the subject of heated dispute and disagreement. Contrary to prevailing American legend, for example, Fernando Orozco, a Mexican historian, asserts that the surviving defenders of the Alamo surrendered, were taken prisoner by Mexican forces, and were executed by firing squad on March 7, 1836. In any event, the military victory by the United States over Mexico resulted in the signing of a peace treaty between two nations: the Treaty of Guadalupe Hidalgo. Pursuant to Article VIII of the treaty, those Mexicans who preferred to remain in the territories that would now be part of the United States had the option of either retaining their status as Mexican citizens or becoming citizens of the United States. Those who remained in the territories for more than one year without having declared an intent to retain Mexican citizenship were considered to have elected to become citizens of the United States. Most of the inhabitants thus elected to become United States citizens. They were not granted citizenship until their respective states were admitted into the union. They were not immigrants; the country, instead, had come to them.

Even when these Hispanics sought to claim citizenship and statehood on a par with other peoples who had entered the Union, they ran into opposition. For example, despite many attempts, New Mexico was not admitted as a state until 1912. National commentators repeatedly and successfully urged opposition to granting statehood to a population "who haven't troubled to learn English." New Mexico's population was characterized by one writer as "half-breeds, greasers, outlaws, etc., . . . no more fit to support a proper state government than . . . to turn missionaries." Another asked whether it would be fair to place "the mixed and half-civilized people of New Mexico on a par with the people of Massachusetts and Wisconsin."[3]

Ironically, while the United States forced both Blacks and Hispanics into the Union, it soon sought to try to devise means of purging itself of most of them. From the beginning, involuntary incorporation meant death for many Blacks and Hispanics, and the resentment by Whites of those who survived and remained.

Benjamin Franklin objected to bringing Africans into the United States, asking, "Why increase the Sons of Africa by planting them in America, where we have so fair an opportunity, by excluding all Blacks and Tawneys, of increasing the lovely White and Red?"[4] In a letter to James Monroe of November 19, 1801, Thomas Jefferson objected to the presence of Africans as a "Blot or mixture on that surface" of the United States. Other White leaders, during the early years of the United States, favored the physical removal of Africans from the United States.

Similarly, throughout the history of this country and especially during this century, many have called for the removal of Hispanics. It may come as a shock to some Hispanics to learn that these calls were made by many people, including noted intellectuals, who recognized the presence of African blood in Hispanics and used that as an important indicator of the need to remove them. The best example can be seen in efforts in the 1920s to curtail Mexican immigration.

In 1921 and 1924 Congress passed immigration laws that for the first time placed numerical limits on the admission of European aliens. However, by 1925 race-conscious nativists realized that Mexico had been excluded from the numerical restrictions. Referring to unlimited immigration from Mexico, Madison Grant, one of America's most influential nativists, argued that "it is not logical to limit the number of Europeans while we throw the country open without limitation to Negroes, Indians, and half-breeds."[5] In their campaign for restriction, nativists stressed racial reasons for excluding Mexicans. Again, referring to Mexicans, Princeton economist Robert Foerster, in a study sponsored by the Department of Labor, noted that mestizo, Indian, and Black stock, that is, Mexicans, "do . . . not attain the race value of white stocks and therefore . . . tend to lower the average of the race value of the white population in the United States" (Reisler, at 153). Foerster insisted that no rational individual could contend that immigrants from below the Rio Grande were "racially better stock" than Europeans. Therefore, "There would appear to be no valid justification for permitting" such persons to continue to enter the United States. We can now, if we desire, recruit our future human seed stock from immigrants of assimilable races, who will also improve our existing hereditary family stock qualities. We can serve and improve our domestic plants and animals, why not our human seed-stock also?" (id.). Historian Albert Bushnell Hart predicted that allowing Mexicans into the United States "will plague future generations very much as the South has suffered from the presence of unassimilable Negroes" (id.).

Besides fearing a booming Mexican birthrate, nativists feared the possibility of miscegenation. Congressmen John C. Box and Thomas A. Jenkins argued that because Mexicans themselves were the product of intermarriage among Whites, Indians, and Blacks, they harbored a casual attitude toward interracial unions and were likely to mix freely with both Whites and Blacks in the United States. To the congressmen, "Such a situation will make the blood of all three races flow back and forth between them in a distressing process of mongrelization. No other alien race entering America, provides an easier channel for the intermixture than does the mongrel Mexican . . . their presence and intermarriage with both White and Black races . . . create the most insidious and general mixture of White, Indian and Negro blood strains ever produced in America."

Nativist Harry Laughlin warned, "If the time ever comes when men with a small fraction of colored blood can readily find mates among White women, the gates would be thrown open to a final radical race mixture of the whole population." "The perpetuity of the American race," he explained, depended entirely upon the "virtue of American women" (id.). Hostility against Mexicans and Mexican Americans, fomented by Laughlin and other nativists, led to the actual deportation of American citizens of Mexican American origin during the Depression.

Of course, not all Blacks and Hispanics were involuntary arrivals in the United States. Even now, voluntary Black immigration, while higher among Hispanics, still accounts for a significant portion of the increase in the Black population in the United States. According to the Census Bureau, one-sixth of the increase in the Black population from 1980 to 1982 resulted from immigration. Among Hispanics, more than half of the increase during this time period occurred as the result of immigration.

It is the dramatic increase in the Hispanic population due to immigration that has led to the projections that Hispanics will soon overtake Blacks as the largest minority group in the country. By 1994, Hispanics outnumbered Blacks in four of the ten largest cities in the United States (Los Angeles, Houston, Phoenix, San Antonio), and were poised to overtake the Black population in the largest city, New York. These numbers led to the projections that the Latino population will surpass that of African Americans sometime around the year 2005.

How then did Hispanics and Blacks get here? They got here the hard way. They were placed in chains, loaded onto ships, hauled across an ocean, and turned out onto plantations. They were conquered, subjugated, and incorporated into a society that needed their labor and resented their presence. They arrived on the East Coast and in the South. They were in the Southwest and West when the Whites arrived. Now, many more of them arrive with the hope shared by all other Americans for a better life for themselves and their children. They meet each other, in increasing numbers, in urban areas throughout the nation. For the first time in hundreds of years they once again share their living and work arrangements. In the process, they are doing what White nativists feared the most: they are mixing their blood with each other, and with Whites.

3 ■ *Who Are We Really?*

I f we are ever effectively to address the Black-Latino conflict, one of the first steps is to abandon the practice of discussing Blacks and Hispanics as though they were mutually exclusive groups. As we have already seen, many if not most Hispanics carry some African blood. As many as 90 percent of African-Americans are of multiracial mixed blood. It makes little or no sense to discuss whether Caribbean immigrants are "Black" or "Hispanic"; many are clearly both.

Unfortunately, it may be human nature for members of an oppressed group to turn their frustration and resentment on another group rather than taking on a powerful oppressor. As a result, some Hispanics, themselves victims of discrimination, look down on African Americans. They may believe they are superior partly because the media constantly reminds them that Hispanics will soon outnumber Blacks. Some African Americans believe the media are identifying Hispanics as a replacement group for Blacks while Blacks are resisting losing the civil rights they acquired after decades of struggle. Seeing Blacks and Hispanics as competing and mutually exclusive groups enhances this view. But the reality is that the identity lines are not as clearly drawn as the media blitz might suggest. Indeed, as will be discussed below, in many instances it is even difficult to define "Hispanic."

This brings us to a second point. The public needs to stop talking about Blacks and Hispanics as if both were monolithic groups of people, both sharing similar if not identical views on race, religion, politics, language, and culture. After all, Africans did not come to America as Africans. Rather, they came as members of distinct tribal groups: Ibo, Wolon, Yoruba, and others. The Hispanic population of the United States is similarly made up of people from a number of countries and may have as many dissimilarities as commonalities.

Why then do these calcified, hard-and-fast categories of race persist? Who determines into what category people fall? Is it genetically accurate or morally appropriate to create and perpetuate these pigeonholes? Does their existence assist or impede solutions to race-related problems in this country?

To answer these questions, let us first consider the history of White immigration to this country. Europeans did not immigrate as "Europeans." Rather, they came as the Irish, as the French, or as the Germans. They brought with them their language, religion, and the customs of their home countries. Contrary to the myth that Europeans immediately immersed themselves in the English language and began speaking English, it took many generations for various European languages to fall into disuse in America. In the early 1900s a bilingual foreman would often appear at an employer's business with a work crew of fellow immigrants. The employer would hire the entire crew, with the foreman serving as interpreter. Eventually, the workers and their children would learn English and the mother tongue would take a secondary but still important role.

Africans, too, arrived speaking no English. They more quickly gave up their native language because of the threats of slave owners not to speak to one another in a native tongue. The slave owners feared that the maintenance of a foreign tongue the Whites could not understand would assist the slaves in plotting rebellion. Contrary to the experience of the Europeans who immigrated to the United States, African Americans could not publish newspapers in their native tongues nor were they allowed to gather in social clubs where the languages could be spoken and passed on. Many slaves took on some of the religious practices of the slave owners. Slaves dressed, ate, and lived according to the dictates of their White owners.

New arrivals, even White arrivals, were never universally welcomed to this country. Bitter anti-Irish rioting occurred on the East Coast of the United States in the late 1800s. Germans were denounced during various periods in United States history, including during the two world wars. Nativists in the early part of the 1900s suggested that Italians and other southern Europeans were genetically inferior and more prone to criminality.

However, all Europeans were identifiably lighter skinned than the slaves brought from Africa. Thus, even though Europeans often arrived not knowing English and sharing religious beliefs different from the majority, their skin color was the critical factor in their ultimate assimilation into White America. The assimilation process required the subordinate group to recognize myths of historical similarities and accept the dominant group's culture and historical predisposition. The assimilation of the Irish in the United States is a classic example of this process. Indeed, despite being despised at first, Irishmen eventually became foremen and then plant owners, and within several generations the Irish were identifiably part of the White majority. The same process occurred with other European immigrants.

The only explanation for the "nonassimilation" of African Americans was their color. After all, African slaves were in no position to perpetuate their own national and tribal identity. They were forced by their social conditions within the Americas to accept their designation as Blacks or Africans. They gave up native languages and religions. Yet they were still not accepted into the body politic in the same fashion as Whites.

The legal emancipation of the slaves did not end the oppression of Blacks, nor did the Constitutional amendments enacted following the Civil War. To help implement legal protections resulting from the post–Civil War amendments, Congress, courts, and legislatures began creating remedies for some of the bitter discrimination Blacks have had to endure. Perhaps the largest strides toward racial equality occurred with the passage of the Civil Rights Act of 1964. However, the remedies being created were aimed primarily at preventing racial discrimination against Blacks. Other racial minorities were simply not seen as a significant segment of society. In the Kerner Commission report released in 1968 about the urban rioting that had swept the nation, the Commission noted: "Our nation is moving toward two societies, one Black, one White—separate and unequal."

Ironically, it may have been the work of this Commission and the civil rights advocates in the 1960s that has led to some of the tension between Blacks and Hispanics. Given the history of slavery and oppression that Blacks have endured, it was logical and just to create civil rights remedies for them, especially since they constituted 10 percent of the population. But now Hispanics are insisting on the benefit of the same laws. Was it the "fault" of Hispanics that they were largely invisible and unprotected during the enactment of the civil rights legislation in the 1960s? Of course not. Hispanics constituted about 4 percent of the population of the United States at that time. Yet they could not even identify themselves as Hispanics in the census. Their oppression, while not of the same character as the legacy of slavery, nonetheless did exist and was largely ignored.

The struggle for the benefits of race-conscious remedies is not limited to competition between Blacks and Hispanics. Even within the Hispanic communities, there is intense disagreement about who should benefit from these remedies. In 1991, for example, Pete Roybal, a native of New Mexico and a veteran of the San Francisco Fire Department, argued against the inclusion of Spaniards in the Hispanic category for purposes of affirmative action before the San Francisco Civil Service Commission. He contended that historically Spaniards have not been among the oppressed; rather, they were responsible for the destruction of the indigenous cultures in Latin America. Others argued in favor of including Spaniards.

Before continuing our discussion of the conflict between Blacks and Hispanics, let us ascertain who is included in each group.

WHO IS "HISPANIC"?

From the previous discussions we have seen that there is no such thing as a Hispanic "race." Hispanics can be found at every point along the spectrum of color. Other than the common reference to Hispanics as "brown," there is no physiological litmus test to define Hispanics in racial terms. Hispanics carry a mixture of Mongoloid, Caucasian, and Negroid blood.

From a sociological perspective it is also difficult to define "Hispanic." After all, the national origins of Hispanics vary. While the Spanish language is one denominator, it is not common to all Hispanics. There are many U.S.-born Hispanics who speak no Spanish. The Spanish spoken in Spain is different from the Spanish spoken within Latin American countries. Words that have a widely accepted meaning in one country can be slang for sexual matters in another. Hispanics tend to be Roman Catholic, but the Roman Catholic church has had a strained relationship with governments in Latin America. In part, this is the result of the church's perceived participation in the oppression of indigenous peoples. It is also the result of the church's alleged distance from the concerns of indigenous populations and in favor of European-oriented Latin American elites. Recently, within the United States, some Hispanics have abandoned the Catholic church and flocked to growing evangelical churches.

In spite of these differences, there are many similarities. The vast majority of Hispanics in the United States, perhaps as many as 70 percent, are Catholic. A comparable number speak Spanish. Another common thread among the various national-origin groups that constitute "Hispanics" in the United States is the lower educational level of most Hispanics compared to Blacks or Whites. As a result, they belong more consistently to a lower socioeconomic level. Most Hispanics who do vote tend to vote Democratic. The percentage of family households in the United States is higher for Hispanics (80 percent) than for either Blacks or Whites (70 percent). Of course, these characteristics do not define a "Hispanic." After all, it is quite easy to identify White or Black individuals or families with these same characteristics and interests. In reality, it appears that the interest in identifying oneself as "Hispanic" arose soon after federal legislation in the 1960s, particularly the Civil Rights Act of 1964, created the possibility for race-based remedies against discrimination. At the same time, an emerging awareness among Hispanics, particularly Chicanos in the Southwest, produced more interest in self-identification as Hispanics.

Nomenclature has always been a problem in this regard. Many Mexican American, Puerto Rican, and Cuban Ameri-

can leaders have denounced the term "Hispanic" as a stereo-
typic label produced in the 1970s by bureaucrats whose purpose was to force diverse peoples and national-origin
groups into one nebulous, overinclusive category. Some social scientists have criticized the term as implicitly under-
scoring the White European culture of Spain at the expense
of the non-White cultures that have shaped Latin America.
Others prefer the term "Latino" as an inclusive term. This
word, too, would obviously refer to a European model because "Latin" originated in Rome. "Latin American" was a
euphemism chosen by assimilationist Mexicans such as the
founding, in Corpus Christi, Texas, in 1929, of the League of
United Latin American Citizens. Virtually every organization of Hispanics wrestles with the nomenclature issue.

Another difficulty has arisen because the problems in
classifying and defining Hispanics are due to the large immigrant population and the different racial classifications
within the countries of origin. Many Hispanic immigrants to
the United States would be considered White in their home
countries. Others would not be, but would choose to self-
identify as White upon arrival in the United States in order
to avoid or seek to avoid discrimination in this country. In
the 1960 and 1970 censuses, more than 95 percent of Latin
American immigrants were classified as White. In 1980, the
Census Bureau expanded its racial classifications allowing
persons to identify themselves as "Spanish." By 1990, the
Census Bureau had eliminated the "Spanish" category, but
many Latin American immigrants continued to classify
themselves as other than Black or White.

Other problems of trying to define a universal "Hispanic" identity revolve around the distinct economic and political differences among Hispanic communities. Many Mexican Americans, for example, can trace their ancestry in what is now the United States back to the time before the arrival of the Europeans. Other Mexican Americans and Mexicans have arrived recently. Mexican Americans are the Hispanic group with the highest proportion of illegals, as well as the highest proportion of native-borns.

Cuban Americans arrived in several waves, beginning with the exodus following Castro's rise to power. The first wave of refugees brought with them material resources and educational accomplishments. Due to the politics of the Cold War, immigrants from Cuba have been treated more favorably by U.S. law than the nationals of just about any other country in the world. Compare the treatment of Cuban refugees with Haitians, for example. Cuban Americans tend to be more prosperous and more Republican than other Hispanics. More recent arrivals from Cuba have not been so prosperous. The Mariel boat lift of the early 1980s brought thousands of impoverished and, in some cases, criminal Cubans to the shores of the United States.

Many Puerto Ricans came to the mainland after having been pushed off the land and out of cities by post–World War II industrialization. Their situation is unique, due to the unusual political relationship with the United States. Puerto Ricans acquire U.S. citizenship at birth; they are not immigrants. Yet they have no voting representation in Congress.

Other Latin American groups have experienced similar differences in history and in economic terms. As a result,

groups of Hispanic immigrants have tended to settle together in distinct regions. Approximately two-thirds of all
Cuban Americans live in Florida. More than two-thirds of
Puerto Ricans live in the northeastern part of the United
States. Almost two-thirds of Mexican Americans live in the
West and Southwest. Even in cities with several Hispanic
groups, new arrivals from each national-origin group tend
to live in distinct areas, apart from other Hispanic immigrant groups.

The political interests of these groups tend to converge
around language-rights issues, voting-rights issues, and bilingual education. But they diverge seriously on other issues. Cuban Americans have long sought strong anti-Cas-
tro initiatives. In August 1993, some Cuban Americans in
Miami burned Mexican flags in protest over the Mexican
government's deportation to Cuba of a group of rafters
who had escaped the island and were driven into Mexico
by storms. The televised images of Cuban Americans burning Mexican flags angered many Mexican Americans in the
United States. Tensions between Puerto Ricans and Mexican Americans escalated in 1994 when the Hispanic National Bar Association headed by Puerto Rican lawyer Wilfredo Caraballo complained that if other Hispanic groups
had backed Judge José Cabranes for appointment to the
Supreme Court, President Bill Clinton would have appointed him instead of ultimately selecting Judge Stephen
Breyer. "He would have had the nomination had he been
of Mexican origin," Caraballo claimed.[1]

The courts have been called upon frequently to try to
determine who is "Hispanic" and whether that person is

entitled to protection under various civil rights statutes. For example, Section 1981 of the Civil Rights Act of 1866 (42 U.S.C. §1981) was passed as part of the post–Civil War legislation to implement protections to be afforded to the newly enfranchised Black citizens of the United States. It reads as follows:

§1981. Equal rights under the law
All persons within the jurisdiction of the United States shall have the same right in every State and Territory to make and enforce contracts, to sue, be parties, give evidence, and to the full and equal benefit of all laws and proceedings for the security of persons and property as is enjoyed by white citizens, and shall be subject to like punishment, pains, penalties, taxes, licenses, and exactions of every kind, and to no other.

Most courts that have decided the question have determined that national-origin discrimination in itself is not covered by the statute. However, where the same discrimination can be characterized as "racial," plaintiffs are allowed to bring suit. In 1977 a Slavic man sued his former employer alleging unlawful national origin discrimination. Ultimately, the U.S. District Court for the Western District of Pennsylvania rejected his claim. In the process, though, the court observed that the terms "race" and "racial discrimination" may be of such doubtful sociological validity as to be scientifically meaningless. The court went on:

Hispanic persons and Indians, like Blacks, have been traditional victims of group discrimination, and, however inaccurately or stupidly, are frequently and even commonly subjected to a "racial" identification as "non-Whites." There is accordingly both a practical need and a logical reason to extend section 1981's proscription against exclusively "racial" employment discrimination to these groups of potential discriminates.[2]

In other cases courts have also concluded that section 1981 should be construed to protect non-Black persons who are the objects of discrimination. Prejudiced persons may perceive such people to be non-White even though such a racial characterization is incorrect. According to this view, prejudice is considered a matter of practice or attitude based on the mistaken concepts of "race." If a group is commonly perceived to be racially different it will be protected regardless of its "objective" racial composition. In one such case, a court determined that this "common perception approach" adapts the statute to the reality of modern America while remaining true to the aim of its framers. In that case, a Mexican American employee of Safeway Stores, Inc., alleged he had been discriminated against because he was of "Mexican American descent." The employer and a labor union, both defendants in the case, moved to dismiss the complaint. A lower court threw out the complaint, but on appeal, the United States Court of Appeals for the Tenth Circuit reinstated it, stating:

If "white citizens" means a race, which technically does not seem particularly clear, it would seem that a group which is discriminated against because they are somehow different as compared to "white citizens" is within the scope of section 1981. We cannot consider this as a "national origin" case and that alone. Prejudice is as irrational as is the selection of groups against whom it is directed. It is thus a matter of practice or attitude in the community, it is usage or image based on all the mistaken concepts of "race."[3]

Another series of protections against racial discrimination is found in the Civil Rights Act of 1964. The congressional debates that led to the passage of this act include obvious reference to the need to protect Hispanics. The terms "Mexican American," "Spanish surname," "Spanish speaking," "Mexicans," "Puerto Ricans," and others were used in the debates. Congressman Edward Roybal of Los Angeles had the following comments by Congressman Gonzalez from Texas placed in the *Congressional Record* of June 15, 1967:

> In the first place, there is the problem of definition. There is not even a generally accepted name for this minority group. Americans of Spanish surname are called Mexicans, Mexicanos, Latins, Latinos, Latin-Americans, Mexican-Americans, and Hispanic-Americans . . . this group of people is so scattered about the land and so disparate in its origins that it has problems defining itself, just as the government has problems in defining it.

As a result, the statutes as ultimately enacted included the protection against discrimination not only on the basis of race or color, but also on the basis of "national origin." Cases determined that national-origin discrimination refers to discrimination due to the country where a person was born, or more broadly, the country from where his or her ancestors came. "Hispanics" were considered to be a protected class under this definition, even though they, and in many cases, their ancestors for many generations, were native Americans.

Perhaps the most widely accepted legal definition of "Hispanic" is found in the official regulations of the United States Equal Employment Opportunity Commission. There, Hispanics are defined to include persons of Mexican, Puerto Rican, Cuban, Central or South American, or of other Spanish origin or culture regardless of race. In implementing these regulations, the EEOC and the courts look primarily to self-identification. On the other hand, some courts have determined that the plaintiffs' discrimination must be based on their objective appearance to others and not on their subjective feelings about their own ethnicity.

An examination of other cases gives differing and sometimes inconsistent definitions of who is "Hispanic" for purposes of civil rights litigation. Among the determinations are "people who have Spanish last names"; "any Spanish-surname person or individual of Hispanic ancestry"; "pertaining to or deriving from the people, speech or culture of Spain or Spain and Portugal, often specifically Latin American." Can persons of European origin qualify as "Hispanics"? Under the EEOC definition, which is the same definition used by the Postal Service in collecting self-identification data since 1980, a person of "Spanish" lineage would indeed be covered.

WHO IS BLACK?

One might initially assume that it is easier to define "Black" than "Hispanic." After all, unlike Hispanics, Blacks who were brought involuntarily to the United States were forced to give up their tribal or national identities. Do not Blacks, more clearly than Hispanics, belong to a separate and distinct "race"? The answer is no. Even though under the "perception" test Whites might say that Blacks look more unambiguously Black than Hispanics look Hispanic, the reality is that up to 90 percent of the Black population of the United States, is in fact, multiracial. Don't Blacks in the United States now share a common national origin? Again, the answer is no, at least as regards Caribbean and Latin American immigrants. Recall that one-sixth of the increase in the Black population between 1980 and 1992 was the result of immigration. Clearly not all Blacks share the same language. Black immigrants from Central and Latin America bring with them the ability to speak Spanish. Brazilians enter this country with the knowledge of Portuguese, and newly arriving Africans bring with them any number of languages and dialects. Black Haitians, who have been much more unfavorably treated in the immigration process than Cubans, bring a variation of French with them. Nor do Blacks share a common religion. While most are Protestant, African Americans are represented in all other major religions in this country.

The influx of immigrants has led to divisions within the Black community just like national-origin rivalries play a large role in Hispanic communities. Some Jamaicans, for example, even though they may be perceived as Black by the White majority, don't consider themselves Black at all. To a West Indian, Black is a literal description: you are black if your skin is black. But if you have a multiracial background, as many from the West Indies do, the identification is not so clear. These differences may be significant. In the past twenty years, a huge number of West Indians have arrived and settled in the New York area. They now number more than half a million and, on average, make substantially more money than American Blacks. The success of these people who would be perceived as Black by the majority may be the result of an elaborate mechanism that Whites have developed for distinguishing between "good" Blacks and "bad" Blacks. This is similar to the process whereby "good" Hispanics can be distinguished by Whites from "bad" Hispanics. It may be that in the view of Whites, West Indians are to American Blacks what Cuban Americans are to other Hispanics. The advantage to racist Whites is obvious; a biased White can condemn Blacks and Hispanics in general, without fear of being tagged a racist, because he or she simultaneously points with approval to the "good" Blacks or Hispanics as an example of the correct application of the work ethic.

In the case of African Americans, this creates a climate reminiscent of the frustration African Americans have felt in dealing with Korean Americans in Los Angeles. Many Korean immigrants bring with them and harbor inaccurate and prejudicial feelings about Blacks gained from the media and movies. Friction and violence between the groups has occurred. All the while, many racist Whites exploit the tension by condemning Blacks and praising the Koreans for their work ethic. In the same fashion, some politicians shed crocodile tears for Cuban boatpeople, while virtually ignoring Haitian boatpeople.

In terms of judicial and legal recognition of Blacks as such, the history of even more overt racism directed against Blacks ironically makes it somewhat easier for Blacks to claim protection under contemporary civil rights provisions. Under the "one drop" rule a person is Black if he or she has at least one drop of Black blood. The rule was created to maximize the number of slaves. An application of the principle that a small portion of Black ancestry allows for official discrimination was set forth in the United States Supreme Court case of *Plessy v. Ferguson* in 1896. In that case, the Court was asked to consider the constitutionality of a Louisiana law that required separate but equal accommodations for "white" and "colored" railroad passengers. The statute provided that train officials were to assign each passenger to "the coach or compartment used for the race to which such passenger belongs." Plessy, who was one-eighth Black but appeared to be White, took a vacant seat in a railway coach reserved for Whites. He refused to give up his seat and was subsequently imprisoned. The Supreme Court of Louisiana held that the statute was valid. Plessy then brought the case to the Supreme Court on a writ of error. The Supreme Court upheld the statute, concluding that the segregationist measures were reasonable. It stated that in determining the question of reasonableness, the state legislature would be at liberty to act with reference to the established usages, customs, and traditions of the people and with the view to the promotion of their comfort. The fact that Plessy was seven-eighths White made no difference; his small portion of "colored" blood enabled the state to treat him differently than White people.

A variation of the "one drop" rule found its way into a Virginia statute prohibiting marriages between Blacks and Whites. It defined "Blacks" as anyone with an "ascertainable" amount of Black blood. (This statute was stricken as an unconstitutional interference with the right to marry by the Supreme Court of the United States in the case of *Loving v. Virginia* in 1967.)

In adopting measures to protect Blacks against discrimination, the majority of the members of Congress and a majority of judges and legislators have adhered to the notion that Blacks are a separately identifiable race. Yet "races" are not separate genetic entities. African Americans are not a race, nor are Chinese or Serbians. Rather, they are largely artificial statistical entities whose composition varies with each new birth or death and who are always "fuzzy around the margins."[4]

Nonetheless, a growing sense of Black pride in the 1960s promoted the acceptance of the "one drop rule" among African Americans. Even African Americans who, because of lighter skin color, could have self-identified and be taken as White began to take pride in an identification with African Americans. As a result, by the time Congress engaged in debates over the enactment of the Civil Rights Act of 1964, self-identification and perception by the majority that a person was not White proved to be the legal test for defining race and color. Unlike the situation with Hispanics, no reported cases could be found where Blacks have attempted to prove that someone else was not Black for purposes of affirmative action or other race-conscious remedies for discrimination.

WHO DECIDES?

There are no absolute standards for determining who is "Black" or "Hispanic." The sociological and legal approaches discussed above involve self-identification and perception by the majority. The latter standard reinforces the White supremacy model: Whites create a system that assimilates other Whites. Whites determine who is not White and therefore not assimilable. Even when laws and customs change and some relief is afforded to the victims of White oppression, Whites remain in the position of determining who is eligible for the relief.

One explanation for the conflict between Blacks and Hispanics, and even within the Hispanic community, over affirmative action entitlements is that many Blacks and Hispanics, without even realizing it, have accepted this model. Rather than resisting the causes of oppression, Blacks and Latinos direct efforts at limiting participation in the remedies to themselves and to those they perceive to be like them. These efforts are divisive and counterproductive. They also ignore the fact that many poor Whites are themselves victims of oppression. The result is that wrongdoers in a position of power have an easier time maintaining the status quo while their victims squabble over the crumbs of relief tossed their way. It is the classic divide and conquer scenario.

Even the self-identification component of determining racial or ethnic identity perpetuates a White supremacy model where minorities are only afforded rigid, narrow, mutually exclusive options for self-identification. Consider the "Spanish-surname" category that was made available to Hispanics in the 1960s. A person whose father was Hispanic but whose mother was Anglo-American would be allowed by the majority to self-identify as Spanish surnamed and therefore be entitled to affirmative action remedies, yet a person whose mother was Hispanic and whose father was Anglo-American could not. Both carried the same percentage of "Hispanic blood." Even now, what box does a Cuban-born, Spanish-speaking person of African ancestry check: Black or Hispanic? If she marries an Anglo-American White man or an Asian man, what box do their children check?

The data on the number of people of mixed race backgrounds are unavailable simply because the majority has chosen to afford these people the option to identify with only one group. How, then, do these people categorize themselves? One recent study suggests that the children resulting from a marriage between a Black person and a White person are usually considered to be Black. Asians and Native Americans in mixed marriages with Whites classify their own children as White almost twice as often as do African American parents in mixed marriages. While 40 percent of Japanese and more than 50 percent of Native American women are interracially married, only about 1 percent of African-American women and 3 percent of African-American men are. Marriage of female African Americans with men of other races is lower than female "outmarriages" for other racial and ethnic groups. Nonetheless, over the last two decades, the rates of intermarriage between African Americans and Whites have increased. The result is that the number of children in families where one parent is White and the other is Black, Asian, or American Indian has tripled from less than 400,000 in 1970 to 1.5 million in 1990. Because the statistics do not always include children born out of wedlock, the actual numbers are probably greater.

Another problem with self-identification as the method for determining racial classification is that it affords cynical Whites the opportunity suddenly to identify as minorities on graduate school admission or scholarship application forms. In a well-publicized event, a Georgetown law student obtained copies of applications from Whites and minorities. He released data which seemed to indicate that minority applicants with lesser qualifications (i.e., scores on the Law School Admission Test and college grades) were being admitted over White applicants with better qualifications. I have personally observed law school applicants who, for the first and probably last time in their lives, claimed minority status on their application form. The result could be that both poor minority and poor White victims of majority oppression would be denied an educational opportunity when the remaining vacancies are filled by these newly self-identified minority applicants.

Another difficulty with trying to apply the two-pronged

test of self-identification and perception arises in a situation where the two conflict. In a 1996 *Harper's* magazine colloquium entitled "Our Next Race Question: The Uneasiness between Blacks and Latinos," Earl Shorris asked Cornel West: "Cornel, are you a Black man?" Cornel West replied, "Yes" (self-identification). Shorris then asked Jorge Klor de Alva: "Jorge, is Cornel a Black man?" The response: "No" (perception). Shorris noted: "Apparently we have something to talk about."

What alternative would exist then to these two traditional ways of determining minority status? One approach would be to have a government-determined classification scheme. The inherent moral problems associated with this approach are alluded to in a recent decision of the Supreme Court of the United States. In the 1989 case of *Metro Broadcasting, Inc. v. FCC,* the Court upheld the constitutionality of minority preferences in awarding of broadcasting licenses. However, in a dissenting opinion, Justice Kennedy quotes Justice Stephens with this concern: "If the national government is to make a serious effort to define racial classes by criteria that can be ministered objectively, it must study precedents such as the First Regulation to the Reich's Citizenship Law of November 14, 1935." He also points to South Africa's 1950 Population Registration Act as further warning of the problems arising when a government attempts to determine the racial classifications of its citizens.

Another approach would be to allow minority people to identify under a "multiracial" heading or something similar. In preparation for the census of the year 2000, the United States Office of Management and Budget is consid-

Demographic Comparison

	Whites	African Americans	Hispanics	Mexican Americans	Puerto Ricans	Cuban Americans	Central & South Americans
Population (in millions)	206.98	30.39	23.38	13.40	2.40	1.05	3.00
Median household income (in dollars), (1992)	32,368.00	18,660.00	22,848.00	23,714.00	20,301.00	31,015.00	N/A
Percentage of households having income of $50,000 or more (1992)	28.90	13.00	15.50	14.89	14.70	27.50	17.50
Percentage of households maintained by families	69.60	70.00	69.32	81.70	77.80	78.80	82.50
Percentage of female-headed households	12.90	43.80	23.81	19.10	43.30	19.40	20.50
Percentage of households owning home	67.50	42.40	42.40	38.90	23.40	43.50	21.50
Percentage completed high school	79.05	66.10	52.30	46.30	52.50	61.00	60.40

Percentage with four or more years of college	22.03	11.30	5.08	3.02	5.33	13.75	12.70
Percentage unemployed	4.70	11.30	9.90	10.40	11.60	8.10	10.30
Percentage living below poverty level	10.04	30.61	28.70	28.10	40.60	16.90	25.40

SOURCE: Various Current Population Reports 1990, except as noted (U.S. Bureau of the Census).

ering adding a "multiracial category" so that "respondents would not be forced to deny part of their heritage by having to choose a single category."[5] The obvious advantage to this approach is that it would allow people of mixed backgrounds to identify as such without having to deny part of their heritage. Among the disadvantages, some argue, is that the creation of this category would dilute the statistical strength of recognized minority groups. This would have a negative impact on electoral representation, affirmative action, federal contracting rules, allocation of government benefits, and other issues (Ramirez, at 47). It might also delay application of civil rights protections to the newly designated multicultural people. Hispanics recall the legacy of litigation necessary to establish their entitlement to protection. Many people would have to relitigate these same issues under the multicultural label.

THE BOTTOM LINE: THERE ARE DIFFERENCES

Regardless of the identification process, Blacks and Hispanics have some serious and basic differences. As the table indicates, there appear to be some serious demographic and statistical differences among Blacks, Hispanics, and non-Hispanics. There are also significant differences among different Hispanic groupings.

These differences may be the result of, or in some cases the cause of, continuing intraracial and interracial conflicts.

It is against this background, as developed throughout these first three chapters, that we now turn to a discussion of specific areas of conflict and cooperation.

4 ■ *Jobs: Competing for a Shrinking Pie?*

One of the most graphic and tragic examples of Black/Latino job confrontation occurred in my hometown of Santa Fe, New Mexico. Santa Fe has long prided itself on its tolerance and diversity. This image was tarnished by events surrounding the hiring and ultimate resignation of an African American, Donald Grady II, as chief of police of the city of Santa Fe.

Before taking office in July 1994, Chief Grady received an anonymous letter. According to Grady, the letter stated that someone of his race did not belong in Santa Fe. The letter was signed "Hispanics of Santa Fe." Unwilling to yield to bigotry, Grady stepped up to the challenge and accepted the job. An indication of the ugliness he would face occurred when, at a public celebration of Grady's hiring, a police officer placed a pubic hair on a piece of cake which Grady ate. Still unwilling to stoop to the level of his detractors, Grady declined to punish the officer. He persisted,

49

making every effort to convey a sense of professionalism. He was convinced that his years of experience in law enforcement would overcome the bias. Surely racism could not prevail among people who themselves had been so affected by it.

The chief's difficulties mounted when in November 1994 he instituted a policy prohibiting the use of "bolo" ties by nonuniformed officers while on duty. Grady indicated the ties were unprofessional. He also believed that they could be unsafe if officers get into a physical struggle. Many Hispanic police officers and members of the community took offense at the directive that precluded them from wearing the traditional Southwestern alternative to the necktie. They cited the ban as an indication of cultural insensitivity on the part of Grady. Were the objections really aimed at a vigorous defense of the bolo?

Disrespect continued to be heaped on Grady. Police officers and citizens alike began a vocal, orchestrated campaign to criticize Grady at every turn. Grady, who had served as chief of the University of New Mexico campus police, and who was completing work toward a Ph.D, was repeatedly accused of being biased against Hispanics, with the bolo tie ban cited as proof. In December 1994 one of Grady's most vocal critics was elected president of the Santa Fe Police Officers Association. After months of public and private condemnation of Grady, the Association's members voted 103–5 in May 1995 to give the chief a vote of no confidence. As a result of the vote, some Hispanic city councilors began to question Grady's leadership, and his administration became the focus of local attention. In newspapers, on radio talk shows, and in public and private gatherings, citizens debated the issues surrounding the embattled chief. In June 1995 Grady supporters published a petition bearing 248 signatures.

In August 1995 the Santa Fe City Council received petitions that organizers claimed contained more than 2,000 signatures calling for Grady's removal. In response, some of Grady's supporters ran a newspaper ad showing the chief, a Ku Klux Klansman, and two hanging bodies. In firm support of the chief, Mayor Debbie Jaramillo, a Hispanic, compared those who spoke against the chief at a City Council meeting to the Klan. Local officials of the NAACP stated that, while they both supported Grady and believed him to be the victim of racial discrimination, they did not approve of the KKK advertisement and rhetoric. Grady's difficulties continued. In January 1996 police union members threatened to sue Grady after the *New York Times* quoted Grady as saying his own officers had made threats against him. In February 1996, this tragic episode concluded with Grady's resignation.

The Grady incident may be more dramatic than most Black/Latino job conflict situations, but unfortunately, it is not isolated. Race-related tensions can become exacerbated at the workplace, particularly where workers feel little possibility of upward mobility, because there is no immediate escape from supervisors or co-workers. The classic approach-avoidance dilemma develops: I need to work to feed myself and to feed my loved ones; I hate the contact with obnoxious supervisors or co-workers necessary to keep the job. There is no immediate solution to the dilemma, so race becomes a surrogate. It may be universal to dislike one's boss or even co-workers. It may be universal, when the boss is racially different, to focus on race as the reason for the dislike rather than on the inherently disproportionate balance of power. Workers depend, whether they like it or not, on the approval of their supervisors for continuation in employment.

Latinos and Blacks suffer higher unemployment rates than Whites. They make less money than Whites. They are often forced to compete against one another for jobs at the lower end of the pay scale. When they do succeed, they are often distrusted even by members of their own group. Minority workers are familiar with the fact that some White supervisors enlist race as a method of control and thereby exacerbate race conflicts. One White supervisor might praise the work of one minority group while disparaging the work of another. Another may suggest to one group that the other is making unfair demands at the expense of the first minority group in hiring, promotion, and related concerns.

Recently, some supervisors have become quite skilled at a more subtle form of race baiting using the language issue. A White supervisor becomes aware that some Hispanics are speaking Spanish to one another. The supervisor is aware that Black employees probably do not speak Spanish. Aware that human nature inclines one to be distrustful of that which one does not understand, the supervisor then suggests that perhaps the Hispanics are talking about the other minority workers. Tensions develop. Conflicts occur between minority group members. At this point, the White supervisor steps in with a solution: the imposition of a speak-English-only rule designed to minimize interracial conflicts at the workplace. The rule makes Hispanics feel resentful and African Americans feel victorious. The real winner, of course, is the supervisor who has effectively pitted one group against the other. In the case of *Garcia v. Spun Steak Co.*, decided in 1993, a San Francisco meat-packing company which employed thirty-three workers enacted just such a rule after an allegation that two Hispanic workers made derogatory comments in Spanish about an African American and an Asian worker. The rule was upheld by the courts. The resentment created by that rule is now felt across the country.

Other areas of conflict include "downsizing." A business determines that it will be necessary to lay off some workers. Who gets to stay, and at what level of pay? The difficult interplay of collective bargaining agreements, state and federal antidiscrimination laws, and economic and political concerns come into play with the unfortunate result that once again Latinos and African Americans are pitted against one another in a struggle to keep the remaining jobs. This scenario is likely to recur in an era of corporate downsizing and mergers.

The strife models are as limitless as the imaginations of those who perpetuate them either intentionally or because of thoughtlessness or insensitivity. The challenge is also to use our imaginations to create models whereby Latinos and African Americans can understand the dynamics of these situations so they can try to resolve them. First, we'll examine the realities of Black and Hispanic poverty and competition for work. Then we'll see what happens when a minority worker makes it into the ranks of management.

FIGHTING (SOMETIMES LITERALLY) FOR A JOB

Blacks and Latinos make only about half as much, on the average, as Whites. According to the 1990 census, the per capita income of Whites in the United States was $15,700. For Blacks it was $8,900 and for Hispanics $8,400. The result is a staggering difference in the poverty rates for these groups. In 1993, only one in seven White families with children were living below the poverty line. However, more than one-third of Hispanic families with children under age eighteen were below the poverty level (34.3 percent) and almost two in five Black families found themselves in the same situation (39.3 percent).

At the same time, the median income of Hispanic households in 1993 dropped to under $23,000, which was the lowest median income level for Hispanic households since 1975. Since 1989, Hispanic median income values have declined an average of $665 per year. Blacks and Latino workers are laid off more often than Whites. In 1994 the U.S. Department of Labor reported that Hispanic workers, particularly immigrants, incurred more involuntary separations than non-Hispanics because they were less qualified and skilled. In 1992, the percentage of 25–34-year-olds who had failed to complete high school was three times higher for Hispanics than the population as a whole. Whereas only 13.5 percent of the U.S. population in this age group had failed to complete high school, more than 41 percent of

Hispanics had failed to do so. Compared with non-Hispanics, Hispanic workers were generally more likely to be younger, to work in less-skilled occupations, and to be employed in industries in which they would be more likely to lose their jobs.[1]

African Americans face similar obstacles. Historically, they have had higher unemployment rates than Whites. According to the U.S. Census, as recently as 1990 only half as many Blacks (11.5 percent) as Whites (22 percent) had four or more years of college. For Hispanics it is less than 10 percent. As a result of chronic unemployment, a "crisis of poverty" continues to bedevil African Americans. In recent years, the African American unemployment rate has been three times that of Whites, as has the percentage of Blacks living below the poverty line. These ratios seem to remain constant, regardless of changes in the economy. For example, in 1983 Black unemployment stood at 19.5 percent compared with 8 percent for Whites. In 1987, the rates were 13 and 5 percent, respectively. By 1989, while overall the unemployment situation improved, the rates were still close to the 3–1 ratio, with Black unemployment holding at 11.6 percent and White at 4 percent. Over the last three decades the poverty ratio has followed this same proportion. In the time period 1970 to 1979, 32 percent of Blacks overall lived in poverty, compared to 9 percent of Whites. During the 1980s the figures were 33 percent and 11 percent, respectively. In 1990, 32 percent of Blacks and 11 percent of Whites lived in poverty.[2]

The causes of Black poverty include factors other than unemployment. Housing segregation is a critical component in maintaining an African American underclass.[3] In the past, "blame the victim" explanations have been offered. In 1965, Assistant Secretary of Labor Daniel Patrick Moynihan identified the disintegration of the Black family as the cause of persistent poverty.

In addition to these reasons, race discrimination has been a powerful factor that has limited educational opportunities for Blacks and Latinos (see chapter 5). Limited education means limited access to employment. The result is that large segments of the Black and Latino communities, living below the poverty threshold and finding little hope for permanent employment, are easily led to blame the other group in the competition for scarce and underpaying jobs. One of the immediate manifestations of the conflict is that Blacks, like other groups in the United States, blame Hispanic immigrants for taking away jobs they feel should go to Black Americans. The NAACP supported the 1986 Immigration Reform and Control Act which, for the first time, made it illegal to hire undocumented workers in this country. A 1980 Roper survey revealed that a slightly greater percentage of Blacks (82 percent) than Whites (80 percent) agreed that the United States should curtail the number of legal immigrants. However, recent research concludes that there is little factual basis for the notion that immigrants have had any significant negative impact on the employment situation of African Americans. Such academic research means little to an African American worker unable to find or retain a decent job while the media and White nativists continue to blame Hispanic immigrants for the lack of employment opportunities. Yet Blacks have been the victims of White job discrimination throughout the history of the United States, even during periods of more modest Hispanic immigration. Traditional American racism would probably still make it difficult for Blacks to find well-paying jobs and earn as much as Whites even if Hispanic immigration were to cease today. Similarly, in areas of the Southwest where there are relatively few Blacks, Hispanic unemployment is dramatically higher than White. It thus seems unlikely that Blacks are taking jobs away from Hispanics in epidemic numbers.

Nonetheless, Blacks tend to blame Hispanics for Hispanic poverty and vice versa. In a 1994 Harris poll, 49 percent of Blacks said that Hispanics "tend to have bigger families than they are able to support." Twenty-six percent of Hispanics agreed that "Blacks want to live on welfare." One in four African Americans agreed that Hispanics "lack ambition and the drive to succeed." Thirty-three percent of Hispanics agreed that "even if given a chance, they (Blacks) aren't capable of getting ahead."

Unfortunately, sometimes the tension and conflict over jobs breaks into open physical conflict. In July 1992, Latino laborers and their White foreman were allegedly attacked and chased off a construction job in Los Angeles by about thirty-five Black men. The action was allegedly part of a "brotherhood crusade" that initiated a highly publicized campaign to close down South Los Angeles construction sites that would not employ Black workers. Black demonstrators had marched several times on building sites and driven off workers, many of them Latinos. In response, Latino leaders indicated that they would organize "sting

teams" of undercover construction workers with video
cameras to monitor work sites employing Latinos in an
effort to identify demonstrators who turn violent. The campaign among minority groups to acquire new employment
opportunities in post-riot South Los Angeles was reported
to be sparking physical violence on the streets.[4]

There are no ready answers to these conflicts. (The last
chapter of this book will identify some methods for accommodation.) The first and foremost key to success involves
education. Yet, as the next chapter indicates, educational
opportunities are becoming more limited for Blacks and
Latinos. Vigorous enforcement of state and federal laws
prohibiting employment discrimination is another obvious
solution. But at this point in our history, we seem to have
lost whatever little will we once had to do that. It may take
a rebirth of Black and Brown consciousness and unity to
force attention to the critical issue of jobs and economic
security.

MOVING ON UP, AND
MEETING RESISTANCE

Despite the obstacles, many Blacks and Latinos are finding
work. Some are breaking into the ranks of management.
These modest civil rights gains in recent decades mean a
greater likelihood that workers will have contact with a
minority supervisor. In March 1995 the federal Glass Ceiling Commission was able to report that Black males held
3.9 percent of all management positions in the public and
private sectors, and Hispanic males held 6.4 percent of
them. Black females held 4.6 percent of the positions and

Hispanic females held 5 percent. Eight percent of these Black managers reported supervising Hispanics and 8 percent of Hispanic managers reported supervising Blacks. Similarly, 15 percent of Black workers had a Hispanic supervisor and 15 percent of Hispanics had a Black supervisor. However, the percentage of Hispanic workers who achieve managerial status is higher than the percentage of Hispanics in the workforce. For Blacks, the opposite is true. Hispanic males account for 6.4 percent of the managerial workers, even though Hispanic males only constitute 4.8 percent of the workforce. The ratio for Hispanic females is similar: 5 percent of managers are Hispanic females while only 3.1 percent of the workforce consists of Hispanic women. On the other hand, while Black men made up 4.73 percent of the workforce, they only accounted for 3.9 percent of the supervisors nationwide. While Black women made up 5.2 percent of the nation's workers, only 4.6 percent of this country's supervisors were Black in March 1995.

Contact with a minority supervisor for the first time can be unsettling to minority and White workers alike. Some minority workers may have implicitly accepted, even though they resent, a model where Whites dominate and minorities are subordinate. When a minority person assumes a supervisory role, the model no longer works. One scholar, Gordon Allport, identified a subtle mechanism whereby a minority person sees his own group through the eyes of the majority or dominant group, and may hold the same prejudices and stereotypes about minority supervisors as many Whites. The assumption may be that the supervisor obtained the position only as the result of affirmative action and really is not competent.

Minority workers' may assume that things will be better or easier with a minority supervisor. Upon hearing derogatory remarks regarding the supervisor by some White co-workers, a minority worker might determine that the minority supervisor really won't be able to exercise as much authority as a White supervisor. The result is that minority and White workers alike display a low regard for the supervisor.

One of my students, a Black former military officer, experienced this phenomenon. In the military, it is not only customary but mandatory to pay respect to an officer by rendering a hand salute. My student found that Black enlisted people quite often would attempt to greet him in the same manner they would greet another enlisted member of the armed forces and would often not render a hand salute. Some would actually go out of their way not to salute him. In one case, as several enlisted men approached, one turned and started walking backwards toward the officer, facing his peers and talking to them. It was obvious they had all seen the Black officer and it was equally as obvious that this one person did not want to salute the officer.

Another anecdote this same student told me involved a friend, an African American, who had taken a new job supervising a section where four or five African Americans worked under him. The supervisor was friendly, talked with his subordinates often, and tried to be of help to them. Unfortunately, they began to take advantage of his interest. They were late for work and gave less than the required effort. When their conduct worsened and the supervisor finally demanded that they improve, one of them filed a complaint against him. He was accused of not doing his job and being unfair. These accounts, while anecdotal, are consistent with the findings of Allport and others that minorities often view their minority supervisor with lesser regard than they would afford a White person in the same role.

Accusations against a minority supervisor often take on a credence that would not be afforded if the supervisor were White. If there is any doubt that White people give at least initial credence to accusations of wrongdoing against minorities, consider the case of the man in Boston who shot his wife and himself and then reported by car phone that he and his wife had been attacked by a Black man. Susan Smith of South Carolina drove her children into a lake while they were strapped inside her car and killed them; she reported that a Black man had abducted them. Obviously, these people could have reported that the crimes where committed by anyone and there would have been a high level of concern. But in these and similar cases, it is likely that a Black man was picked because a stereotype of Black men as criminals makes an accusation of wrongdoing against a member of that group more believable.

Other problems may develop because a minority supervisor may bring feelings of uncertainty to his or her new role. Feeling a need to establish himself or herself, the supervisor may approach the role in a relatively heavy-handed fashion. The supervisor might feel the need to create a distance from minority workers in order to avoid allegations of favoritism. Or, he or she may pander to existing racial conflicts in order to gain the favor of White workers and supervisors. Virtually everyone criticizes their bosses. Overhearing some criticism, a new minority supervisor may overreact and assume that the criticism is rooted in race. Or hearing a clearly identified racial attack, he or she may choose to underreact and ignore a problem. The offending worker then becomes emboldened and increases the attacks to the point where they become unmanageable.

There are unlimited possibilities of racial strife revolving around management problems. Some of the recurring patterns are represented in the two workplace scenarios that follow. Each is a composite of real life occurrences. Each could offer a beginning point for early identification and resolution of workplace difficulties for Blacks and Latinos.

In the first situation, a Hispanic has worked for years alongside his father in a meat packing plant. He follows his father's advice and attends community colleges and a local university to complete a bachelor's degree in management. Aware of the dedication that the young worker has shown to his work and to his family, the manager of the plant offers him a chance to become assistant manager. His father beams with pride.

For the first month or so things seem to be going well in the newly acquired managerial role. Once or twice, however, the supervisor finds himself in the somewhat uncomfortable role of having to discipline Hispanic co-workers with whom he has grown up. Additional problems begin to surface, and one day the plant manager calls him into his office. "You're doing a good job," the plant manager tells the new supervisor. "But we've got some complaints that you are being too soft on the Mexicans and that you're letting a Black man get away with not pulling his weight. Because I don't want any problems, and because we're going to follow a chain of command here, I've told the workers that they need to speak directly to you." The next day, the Hispanic supervisor calls in the White workers who had complained. He knows the guys and has heard their racially derogatory comments directed against Blacks and Hispanics in the past. He also knows that they are on very good terms with management because they are very productive workers. There is tension as he meets with them.

"We can understand why you're cutting those Mexicans some slack," one of the workers indicates. "But you're letting that lazy 'n——' get away with murder." The Hispanic supervisor indicates that he will resolve the problem. The next day he calls the Black worker to his office. He hands him a copy of a formal reprimand which is being placed in the personnel file. When the Black worker reads the reprimand he becomes furious and says, "You don't treat your Mexican friends this way. Putting you in that office sure went to your head."

"You better watch your mouth," the supervisor snaps.

By this time the raised voices are attracting the attention of the nearby workers. "I'm not going to watch my mouth. I'm telling you this is wrong. You're only doing this to me because I'm Black."

"No", the Hispanic supervisor yells, "I'm only doing this because you're a lazy n——."

All the workers who overhear the conversation, both White and Hispanic, smirk. The Black worker files a complaint with the Equal Employment Opportunity Commission. As part of the settlement, the Hispanic supervisor is removed from his position. He quits, eventually moving his family and finding work in the business office of another firm where he has no supervisory responsibilities.

In the second scenario, an African American woman is employed as a midlevel supervisor by a state agency in the Northeast. Even though she holds a bachelor's degree and has many years of supervisory experience within her own agency, she has had a great deal of difficulty being taken seriously by other supervisors. She has long felt that even though she has more education and training than most other managers within her agency, her appointment was made to satisfy concerns that there be at least one African American supervisor in her region.

Under the rules of her agency, when an employee applies for a supervisory position, a three-person selection team is impaneled to make the final choice. Consistently, the Black supervisor would be placed on the panel and consistently she would be outvoted by the two White supervisors. As a result, she felt increasingly frustrated and unable to help other African American workers become supervisors themselves. When she voices her concerns to the state central office, a region-wide discussion is held. Other White supervisors in her office appear surprised and indicate that they, of course, will be sensitive to assisting in the process of identifying and promoting qualified Blacks.

Soon thereafter, one of the White supervisors invites the

Black supervisor to lunch. "You didn't need to cause such a fuss, we can work these things through together," she indicates. The Black supervisor thanks her. "No, I'm serious. There will soon be three new supervisory openings within our region. I know that you have an African American friend who has been turned down before and this may be his chance."

Soon thereafter, promotion opportunities are posted, including the three that were the subject of the lunch conversation. One of the applicants is an African American who is a friend of the Black supervisor. The Black supervisor is named to all three selection panels. Two other White co-supervisors, including the woman who took her to lunch, are also selected for the panels. When the first position is determined, the Black supervisor votes for her friend. To her surprise, the two White women vote for him as well and he is confirmed. The Black supervisor concurs with her two co-supervisors on the other two positions, which are offered to White employees. One of the applicants who does not get a position is a Latino. He happens to be friends with the African American who is selected for the first supervisory position. When the unsuccessful Latino applicant meets with his friend, the Black applicant tells him, "Hey, don't get discouraged. It's just politics. I can help you out the next time around."

"What do you mean?"

"Well, my friend who is Black cut a deal for me. I got in but she had to vote for the Whites including the White that got your job. Maybe next time she can cut you a deal." The Hispanic is furious and files a discrimination claim against the Black supervisor and her two co-supervisors who made the selection.

The examples of frustration and resentment arising in the context of Black/Latino management conflicts are endless. Some minority managers will fail because they are incompetent. Many more of them will fail because of the prejudice and lack of support they encounter among their co-workers and their supervisors alike. Each failure gives bigoted people the opportunity, the next time a suggestion is made to hire a minority supervisor, to reply with the "Well, you remember what happened when we hired so-and-so" defense. The failings of one manager, whether they were his or her fault in the first place, become the failings of his or her entire racial group. Some models for accommodation will be discussed in the last chapter of this book. Some might work and others won't. In the meantime, the challenge facing all minority workers may be to lift their eyes from the crumbs scattered on the floor and look squarely into the eyes of those feasting at the banquet table.

5 ■ *Education: A Crumbling Commitment*

This chapter is filled with a lot of bad news. Both Blacks and Hispanics have had a long and painful history trying to obtain educational opportunities equal to those of Whites. Even modest gains have been thwarted as the courts, politicians, and the phenomenon of White flight to the suburbs combine to snatch away crumbs of educational opportunities. We are resegregating our public schools. We hear new calls to ban undocumented children from the schools. And, as in other areas, Blacks and Latinos find themselves confronting each other over the diminishing opportunities to obtain quality educations for their next generations. We will approach these topics by first considering the separate experiences of Blacks and Hispanics, because for the largest part of the history of this country, that is exactly how Black and Hispanic children have been educated: separate from each other and separated from Whites.

THE BLACK EXPERIENCE: SEGREGATION, INTEGRATION, RESEGREGATION

Slave owners recognized that education was utterly incompatible with slavery. So fearful were they of the threat to the institution of slavery that they prevented, upon pain of law, the teaching of the slaves by Whites. Frederick Douglass acknowledged both the debt he owed to the White children who taught him to read, and the tremendous risk they ran in teaching him, when he wrote:

> I am strongly tempted to give the names of two or three of those little boys, as testimonial of the gratitude and affection I bear them; but prudence forbids; not that it would injure me, but it might embarrass them; for it is almost an unpardonable offence to teach slaves to read in this Christian country.[1]

Following the Civil War, Blacks in the South were grudgingly afforded very limited access to segregated public schools. While northern Blacks found marginally better educational opportunities, they too were often relegated to second-class facilities and taught away from Whites. In the South, though, segregation was the law of the land. A series of laws mandated that Blacks be separated from Whites not only in the schools, but in public and private accommodations.

In 1896 the Supreme Court upheld these segregationist laws, ruling in the case of *Plessy v. Ferguson* that the state of Louisiana could require that Blacks ride separately from

Whites on the railways. "Equal but separate" treatment of the races would be legally permitted until 1954.

In that year the Supreme Court of the United States handed down its landmark decision in the case of *Brown v. Board of Education of Topeka.* Striking down a line of precedent dating back to *Plessy,* the Supreme Court determined in *Brown* that separate educational facilities are inherently unequal. A unanimous Supreme Court ruled that the maintenance of segregated schools violated the Equal Protection guarantee of the Constitution of the United States. In reaching its decision, the Court concluded that "separating children solely on the basis of race generates a feeling of inferiority that may affect children's hearts and minds in a way unlikely ever to be undone."[2] One year after *Brown,* the Supreme Court ruled that school districts must admit Black students "with all deliberate speed" and ordered the federal courts to continue their jurisdiction over these cases. By 1964, only 2 percent of Black children in the South were attending schools with Whites. Eventually, the Court determined that "the time for mere 'deliberate speed' has run out," and in 1971 the Court ruled in *Swann v. Charlotte-Mecklenburg Board of Education* that the federal courts could order bussing to desegregate public schools.

For civil rights advocates, these dramatic pronouncements by the Supreme Court seemed to herald the dismantling of an apartheid educational system that had relegated black students to a position of bitter inferiority. However, people in this country have freedom to move. Whites took advantage of that freedom by fleeing to the suburbs, away from majority-Black inner-city schools. In the early 1970s, with the flight of White children to the Detroit suburbs, a federal court ordered the city of Detroit to integrate its schools with those of fifty-three suburban school districts. This time, the Supreme Court overturned the order. It held in the case of *Milliken v. Bradley* that school districts in the suburbs could not be ordered by the federal courts to participate in the desegregation of an inner-city school system unless those suburban districts had been illegally involved in the initial segregation.

White flight to the suburbs continued. The phenomenon led the Kansas City school board in 1976 to sue suburban school districts in the state of Missouri, arguing that they had participated in a scheme of encouraging White flight, thus confining Blacks to a deteriorating inner-city Kansas City school system. They argued that even after the *Brown v. Board of Education of Topeka* decision, the State of Missouri had allowed local school boards the discretion of retaining desegregation. Many of the suburban districts around Kansas City denied Blacks admission to public high schools. As a result, Black families were forced to moved into Kansas City so that their children could graduate. The district judge who heard the case dismissed the suburban districts from the case because of the *Milliken* case. But he then determined that the state and the school board had violated the Equal Protection guarantees of the Constitution of the United States. To remedy the racial imbalance, he ordered the renovation of fifty-five schools and the construction of seventeen new ones. When the school district failed to pay its share of the cost, the judge ordered the doubling of the local property tax. However, in 1995 the Supreme Court of the United States overturned the judge's decision. The Supreme Court determined that a district judge has no authority to order the state and a school district to pay for plans aimed at attracting suburban White students back into the public school systems. In a concurring opinion in that case, *Missouri v. Jenkins,* Justice Clarence Thomas, the lone Black Justice, added his weight to maintaining the segregation: "The Constitution does not prevent individuals from choosing to live together, to work together, or to send children to school together, so long as the state does not interfere with their choices on the basis of race." The result is that once legally enforced segregation is eliminated, school districts are permitted to run schools that happen to be all Black or all White.

This is extremely disheartening to advocates who urge, as they did in the early 1950s, that the maintenance of all White and all Black schools generates a feeling of inferiority in the minority children and results in diminished resources to the predominantly Black schools. The lofty promise of desegregation in the *Brown* case has vanished; three-fourths of Latino students and two-thirds of African American students now attend schools that are predominately minority schools. In America's largest cities, fifteen out of every sixteen Black and Latino students are in schools where most of the students are non-White.

There are several explanations for the reemergence of segregation. First and most obvious is the White flight phenomenon discussed above. Another theory is the notion that minorities prefer to cluster in neighborhoods with others of similar racial backgrounds. This clustering is attributable either to choice or to subtle and overt forms of discrimination that have herded them into the ghetto. Government inaction has also contributed to resegregation. Activists urge that without federal government prodding and direct and forceful intervention, local school districts will inevitably resegregate. The reality is that most Whites would prefer not to send their children to school with substantial numbers of minority children. Certainly all of these factors have contributed to the frustration that minority parents encounter in trying to place their children into integrated schools. The process is like a child trying to catch a frog. He approaches slowly, and reaches out, only to watch the frog jump out of reach. He approaches again, and the same thing happens, over and over. Minority parents often lack the resources to keep chasing Whites around the urban and suburban school districts. Even when they do, White parents move their kids into private schools. Affluent Whites then vote against the tax increases necessary to maintain quality education for the remaining minorities and lower socioeconomic White students in the public schools.

But is all segregation bad? Is it true that all Black children who are kept away from White children suffer? Some national studies suggest that desegregation raises the test scores of Blacks.[3] Other studies contradict these results. But beyond test scores, many educators are concerned that depriving inner-city poor children from social contact with middle-class children deprives them of tremendous networking and life experience opportunities which affect the careers and lives of these children down the road.

One emerging phenomenon is that of voluntary segregation. Recent years have seen a trend to establish all-Black public schools with an African-centered curriculum. Such schools now exist in a number of U.S. cities. Their proponents believe that stressing Black history and achievement bolsters the esteem of Blacks by giving them positive role models. It eliminates the intimidation and oppression that Black children may encounter in a predominately White school. Even more controversial is the notion that Black children are cognitively different from White children and different learning techniques can be employed in an all-Black school to the benefit of those children.

Historically Black colleges and universities have long offered an alternative to Black students. Those institutions arose during mandatory segregation as a solution to providing separate but equal education to Blacks. In 1990, these institutions awarded 33 percent of all undergraduate degrees earned by African Americans. In the last decade, they have been the source of nearly half of the nation's Black Ph.D.s, 80 percent of Black lawyers and judges, and 85 percent of Black physicians. At the same time, these institutions do not practice race discrimination. One-fifth of all students attending these historically Black colleges and universities are not Black. Ironically, notwithstanding the success of these institutions, the Supreme Court of the United States is threatening them. In 1992 the Court held in the case of *United States v. Fordyce* that a state university has not successfully integrated if it still maintains practices that are traceable to official segregation and lack educational justification. The Court went on to determine that if a practice can be traced to the era of mandated segregation, and if that practice results in racially identifiable institutions, the state must prove that the practice is justified and cannot be practically eliminated. Some perceived in this a threat to historically Black colleges and universities. That is, if the school existed during the era of official segregation and is a vestige of a university system traceable to the days of segregation, the Black institution would have to prove a sound educational justification to maintain its existence.

Any number of sound educational justifications could meet this test. One is the intellectual experience that can be gleaned from an institution's distinctive history, traditions, prestige, faculty, administrators, and influential alumni. A second justification relates to the ability of these institutions to educate Black students more effectively than predominantly White schools. Black students in these institutions have displayed more positive psychological adjustment and greater cultural awareness than those on predominantly White campuses. Black students at these institutions do not carry the stigma that results when Blacks are required to attend all-Black schools. The power to choose to attend college with one's minority peers eliminates the badge of inferiority that inevitably follows forced White-imposed segregation.

Probably the most important benefit of voluntary segregation is that it promotes pride in racial and ethnic identity. Students enroll at these schools because they *want to.* Even in the public schools, where the issue of choice is not so clear-cut, parents report improved self-esteem among their children through participation in African-centered programs of study. If voluntary segregation does not make minorities feel inferior, then maybe the *Brown* decision has lost some of its rationale. Separate is only inherently unequal when minorities are required by a dominant majority to be separate.

However, disadvantages to voluntary segregation exist. African-centered education can run the risk of being jingoistic. It may not truly prepare Black children scholastically to compete in a still Eurocentric world and workplace. Further, voluntary segregation certainly plays into the hands of Whites who urge a separation of the races. It removes from Whites the opportunity to have their children live and play among minority children. It is always harder to maintain prejudice against a group when you have positive relationships with members of that group. Conversely, prejudice hardens in the absence of experience that contradicts it. In this vein I am reminded of a conversation I had with a well-intentioned White person in a Midwestern state several years ago. Upon learning that I was born and raised in the multicultural environment of Santa Fe, New Mexico, she inquired, "Did you ever know any Native Americans growing up there?" When I answered, "Yes," she asked, "What were they like?" I thought of friends, kids I liked and others I hated and fought with. I remembered girls I dated. I couldn't even begin to recall all of the contacts I had had with Native Americans. I really couldn't think of any generalizations that would satisfy her inquiry as to what Native Americans "were like." They were like me. They were like the woman asking me the question. There were some differences in language and dress and culture but I couldn't tell her simply "what they were like." Similarly, I am certain that there are many Whites whose children will never know "what Black people are like." Their children will never have the chance to play with, love, fight with, and go through life's childhood experiences with Black or Brown children. They will be poorer and less educated for it.

HISPANICS: TRACKING AND EXCLUSION

Although it is less widely acknowledged, Hispanics, particularly Mexican Americans in the Southwest, have faced segregation in the public schools. The difference between this Hispanic experience and that of African Americans is that the segregation of African Americans was largely dictated by state law. For Hispanics, while state statutes would not expressly authorize the segregation of Mexican Americans, local school districts employed a number of mechanisms to accomplish the same result. Just like their Black counterparts, Mexican Americans resisted this segregation, seeking relief in the courts.

One of the first reported cases arose in the city of Del Rio, Texas. That city operated a "Mexican" elementary school that was used exclusively for teaching children of Mexican descent. Parents sought to enjoin this segregation. In 1930, the Texas Court of Civil Appeals held that the schools could not arbitrarily segregate Mexican American children solely because of their ethnicity. However, the court then went on to conclude that the reasons that the district gave for the segregation were legitimate. Linguistic difficulties and starting school late because of migrant farm working justified placing Mexican American children in a segregated school. In 1947, though, the federal courts determined, in a case arising in California, that the segregation of Mexican American students violated the Fourteenth Amendment to the United States Constitution. The courts held that cases, including *Plessy,* that had upheld segregation based on legislative acts did not apply because the California legislature had not authorized the segregation of Mexican American students.

Mexican American parents continued to challenge segregation of their children in the courts. Following the *Brown v. Board of Education of Topeka* case, parents were successful in dismantling systems that arbitrarily assigned their children to "Mexican" schools. However, while the school districts could no longer segregate Mexican American children into separate schools on the basis of ethnicity, school districts in the Southwest developed "tracking" as another method of segregation of Hispanic students. That is, even within an integrated school, Hispanic children were placed in a lower-achieving classroom due to supposed or real language difficulties. In a case entitled *Hernandez v. Driscoll Consolidated Independent School District,* decided by the United States District Court for the Southern District of Texas in 1957, Mexican Americans claimed that the school district violated their constitutional rights by the maintenance of such separate classrooms for children of Mexican descent in the first and second grade. The school district also required a majority of the Hispanic children to spend three years in the first grade before promotion to second grade. The court held that language handicaps *could* justify segregation into separate classrooms but *only* after a credible examination of each child by the appropriate school official.

A dramatic rise in the Spanish-speaking population, particularly in school age children following World War II, had led to renewed debate over the education of language-minority children in the public schools. Not only were foreign languages ignored in the curriculum, Hispanic children were often physically punished for speaking Spanish at school. Other indicators of second-class status were communicated to Hispanic students. A distinguished New Mexico jurist, for example, recalls that he and other Hispanics were marched to the school's showers each day. His English-speaking Anglo-American peers were not.

In the 1960s, civil rights organizations and others sought federal legislation that would guarantee respect for a Spanish-speaking child's cultural heritage while at the same time enabling the child to gain further proficiency in both Spanish and English. They were joined by those who saw bilingual education as the most effective method for producing English-proficient children among language-minority populations. The congressional response was the Bilingual Education Act of 1968. The Act provided grants to promote research and experimentation for meeting the needs of children who demonstrated little or no proficiency in the English language. In 1970, the Health Education and Welfare Department of the United States enacted a regulation pursuant to Title VI of the Civil Rights Act of 1964. The Civil Rights Act of 1964 provides in part,

> No person in the United States shall, on the basis of race, color, or national origin, be excluded from participation in, be denied the benefits of, or be subjected to discrimination under any program or activity receiving federal financial assistance.

The 1970 regulation, enacted pursuant to Congressional power under the Civil Rights Act, provided,

> Where inability to speak and understand the English language excludes national origin minority group children from effective participation in the educational program offered by a school district, the district must take affirmative steps to rectify the language deficiency in order to open its instructional program to these students.

In 1982, the United States Congress passed the Equal Educational Opportunity Act. Included in the provisions of that law is the following:

> No state shall deny equal educational opportunity to an individual on account of his or her race, color, sex, or national origin, by . . . the failure by an educational agency to take appropriate action to overcome language barriers that impede equal participation by its students in instructional programs.

A number of states also enacted their own bilingual education provisions. However, up to this point, the courts have not recognized a constitutional right to education, let alone a right to bilingual education.

Not everyone is content with even the limited right to bilingual education in this country. Indeed, some have urged the exclusion of undocumented Hispanic children from the public school systems altogether. One such impulse was a law enacted in May 1975 by the Texas legislature. The law withheld from local school districts any state funds for the education of children who were not "legally admitted" into the United States. It also authorized local school districts to deny enrollment in the public schools to these children. When a challenge to this law reached the Supreme Court of the United States in 1982, the Court ruled the law unconstitutional. It determined that even though there is no constitutional right to an education, where the state provides public schooling it cannot, consistent with the Equal Protection clause of the Fourteenth Amendment, deny access to those schools to children who are not legally admitted into the United States. The court's opinion expressed concern about the creation of an underclass that could result from the exclusion of these children. It also noted that "visiting condemnation on the head of an infant is illogical and unjust." Unfortunately, the issue has not been laid to rest by the Supreme Court. Today, new calls are being heard for federal legislation that would give states the right to exclude undocumented children from the public school system. These measures are cruel. Children have no choice over where their families will live. Most of these children will continue to live, with or without formal education, in the United States. Removing them from our schools will not remove them from the United States. Rather, it will create an underclass of uneducated, resentful people. Even at the height of segregation, White supremacists acknowledged a need to provide a separate education for the Black children with whom they did not want their children to associate. We have turned the clock back, with calls to exclude undocumented children from our schools, to the days of slavery. Educators who, in the face of a law prohibiting the education of undocumented children, nonetheless allow them into their classrooms, will run the risk of the White wrath Frederick Douglass wrote about in the pre–Civil War era.

Even when Blacks and Latinos overcome the hurdles and are able to enroll in a quality public school, the factor of unequal enforcement of discipline causes additional problems. Both Hispanics and Blacks receive more discipline than White students. In a school district with both Black and Hispanic presence, according to one study, punishment will first be focused on Blacks and then on Hispanics. As the number of Black student suspensions rises, the number of Hispanic suspensions falls. This finding implies that not only is race a consideration when dispensing discipline, but there is a trade-off of punishment between one minority group and another. It appears that school administrators compensate for disciplining Blacks by lessening the discipline of Hispanics. This type of unfair treatment can only enhance the conflict between Blacks and Hispanics.

AFFIRMATIVE ACTION AND
HIGHER EDUCATION

Blacks and Latinos continue to be grossly underrepresented in colleges and graduate schools and in the white-collar professions. Modest attempts to undo some of the lingering effects of past discrimination and to create a more diverse educational environment for the benefit of minorities and Whites alike have been met with intense opposition. Historically, graduate and professional schools have given preference to the sons and daughters of their alumni or their contributors. Whites have never challenged this type of "affirmative action." It is only when an institution responds to the reality that there are lingering effects of race discrimination and offers a small number of minority students an opportunity to receive an education that litigation results.

Such was the situation in the case of *Regents of the University of California v. Bakke.* In that case, a White medical school applicant sued the University of California at Davis Medical School after he was denied admission. The medical school had maintained a special admissions program whereby sixteen of the one hundred entering seats were reserved for minority students. Bakke alleged that this program operated to exclude him on the basis of his White race. When the case reached the Supreme Court of the United States, the Court was divided. Four justices found the program unconstitutional. Four did not. Justice Lewis Powell provided the swing vote. He concluded that the particular program was not sufficiently tailored. He determined that every applicant must be able to compete with every other applicant. As a result, in a 5–4 decision, the Supreme Court ruled that the program was unconstitutional. Nonetheless, Justice Powell granted that race *could* be used as a positive factor along with other factors, to determine admissions in order to achieve a diverse student body.

In 1996, the Fifth United States Circuit Court of Appeals, with jurisdiction over lower federal courts in Texas, Louisiana, and Mississippi, went even further. It determined that race could *not* be taken into account in any admissions program. In that case, *Hopwood v. Texas*, four White applicants sued the University of Texas, claiming that its law school discriminated against them in denying their admission to the law school based on race. The University of Texas School of Law had been using an admissions process that separated Black and Hispanic applicants from White applicants. Minority applicants were reviewed separately and minorities with lower scores on the Law School Admission Test were admitted. By the time the case reached the Fifth Circuit, the university had abandoned this system. Nonetheless, the court heard the appeal and used the case to gut affirmative action programs. Ignoring Justice Powell's opinion in *Bakke* that race could be taken into account, the Fifth Circuit Court of Appeals concluded that the University of Texas School of Law could *not* use race as a factor even if it sought to achieve a diverse student body, or to combat a perceived hostile environment. Neither could the university use race-based admissions to enhance the school's poor reputation among minorities, nor even to eliminate any present effects of past discrimination by any institution other than the law school.

In July 1996, the Supreme Court of the United States declined to hear an appeal of the *Hopwood* case. This was good news for civil rights advocates nationwide who feared that the effects of the *Hopwood* decision would apply nationwide if the Supreme Court were to uphold the decision of the Fifth Circuit. On the other hand, for those living within the Fifth Circuit, affirmative action in higher education has essentially ended, at least until the Supreme Court hears such a case and overrules the *Hopwood* principle. The concern was enhanced when the attorney general of the state of Texas announced that he believes *Hopwood* applies to private as well as public institutions, and applies to scholarship decisions as well as to admissions.

Should race be a factor in admissions decisions? Is "merit" the only legitimate criteria? What is merit? Is it only the composite of scores on a multiple-choice admission test and grades in school? Or does it also involve such considerations as a person's character, an ability and willingness to struggle to overcome adversity, a willingness to provide services to a minority community, a willingness to help other minorities overcome a history of segregation and discrimination, and the contributions that an individual's own life experiences can bring to a profession?

Blacks and Hispanics tend to score lower than Whites on the standardized tests used as admissions criteria, tests not surprisingly designed and written by Whites. Many have challenged an inherent cultural bias in the tests. Even the administrators of the Law School Admission Test caution that it cannot and should not operate as the sole criterion in admissions decisions. Yet Whites consistently point to the scores on these tests as proof of reverse discrimination when minorities with lower scores are admitted. These tests do not measure motivation and character. They do not measure other qualities, including general intelligence, that might legitimately serve as an admission criterion. Whites hold a grossly disproportionate number of professional degrees. Unless we believe that the ability to practice law or other professions inherently resides in Whites to the exclusion of most minorities, we would have to conclude that the traditional admissions criteria have excluded minorities on the basis of their race and culture.

There are many well-reasoned defenses of affirmative action. An examination of all of them is beyond the scope of this book. However, as an educator, I offer several brief observations for the continuation of affirmative action in higher education. First, college graduates participate in leadership roles. They have much greater influence in the economic and political system than those without college degrees. They, in turn, act as role models for younger minority students who otherwise might be discouraged from pursuing higher education.

Second, White students, for their own growth as educated people and as human beings, must come to recognize that the professions and leadership roles are open to all people. White students must be able to interact with people from many differing backgrounds if they are to be successful after graduation. The world is, after all, not a college. Enrolling more minority students increases the likelihood of that interaction. Also, a diverse student body is more likely to question assumptions that otherwise might go unchallenged. Diversity, then, is beneficial to White as well as non-White students.

Third, and perhaps most importantly, colleges and graduate schools by the very makeup of their student bodies must signal that they are committed to integration. They must demonstrate that they will not tolerate racism. Their example should encourage students to strive to eliminate the evil of racism from society when they leave the protected walls of academia.

It should only be fair then, as a matter of universities' affirmative action policies, as a matter of law, and as a matter of basic justice, that colleges and graduate schools make the leadership opportunities resulting from higher education available to all segments of society. They must recognize that, in addition to grade point averages and standardized test scores, an important criterion for determining whether a particular applicant should be accepted to the student body must include whether the admission of that applicant would increase or decrease the likelihood that the student body accurately reflects the population as a whole. The ability to successfully complete higher education does not inherently reside in Whites to a greater degree than non-Whites. Institutions, particularly public institutions, cannot continue to rely on the goodwill and tax support of the general population, and at the same time, turn out graduates who disproportionately represent only one segment of that population.

Some remain content with the underrepresentation of

minorities in higher education and in the professions, content to perpetuate the lingering effects of discrimination in elementary and secondary schools. Judges have laid down more obstacles in the path of minority children by making it more difficult for them to gain admission to college and scholarships to finance their educations. Those who succeed in running this gauntlet are going to be superstars. Let us hope they will use their talents wisely and help lift the judicially sanctioned burdens from some of their peers.

CONFRONTATION OVER
RACE-BASED SCHOLARSHIPS

In terms of relations between Blacks and Hispanics, I may have saved the worst news of this chapter for the end. Even where Blacks and Latinos have successfully run the gauntlet of segregation and lifted themselves into a position where they qualify not only for admission but for the possibility of a race-based scholarship, it is not only Whites who will use the courts to deny them that opportunity. In a case with potential far-reaching impact, a Hispanic student successfully sued the University of Maryland to block its awarding of a scholarship aimed at benefiting African Americans. In that case, *Podberesky v. Kirwan,* a Hispanic student was admitted to the University of Maryland and applied for the university's Banneker Scholarship, a scholarship limited to African Americans. The university had established the scholarship partially to counteract its historical discrimination against African Americans, which had resulted in a poor reputation for the university within the African American community. The scholarship was intended, in part, to alleviate this poor reputation. The university also acknowledged that a hostile campus environment was directed toward Blacks. Further, the retention rates for African Americans were lower than for Whites because Black students were more likely to have to provide for their own expenses. Blacks had little time for campus activities and friends because of off-campus work and living arrangements. The university also hoped that the scholarship would help alleviate the underrepresentation of African Americans at the university by bringing in "high-achieving" Black students who would enhance the school's reputation and thus attract more African Americans.

Podberesky met all the requirements except that he did not meet the qualification of being African American. He fell just shy of meeting the academic requirements of another scholarship under the Francis Scott Key program, which is not restricted to African Americans. He sued, challenging the constitutionality of the Banneker scholarship and ultimately won his case. The U.S. Fourth Circuit Court of Appeals emphasized that using race as a remedy may perpetuate the very race-consciousness the remedy is trying to overcome. The court dismissed the university's justifications. It concluded that race could not be a factor in determining Podberesky's qualifications for the scholarship because the program was not narrowly tailored and did not pass the "strict scrutiny" analysis. Because the Supreme Court of the United States declined to review the case, the effect of the *Podberesky* decision is unclear nationwide. To add to the confusion, the United States Department of Education adopted policy guidelines that apply to minority-targeted financial aid. Those guidelines *do* allow race-targeted aid as a remedy for past discrimination or as a tool to achieve a diverse student body.

One of the tragic factors in the *Podberesky* case is that it is another case of in-fighting over crumbs. Nationwide, at the undergraduate level, scholarships for which minority status is the only requirement represent less than one-fourth of one percent of all scholarship money. Only about 3 percent of all undergraduate scholarship money is available where minority status is one of several requirements. The United States Department of Education estimates that only 40 cents out of every $1,000 of federal education assistance funding is devoted to minority-targeted scholarships.

Individual battles between minority students over university resources are not the only points of contention between Black and Latino students. In a number of public schools, Blacks and Hispanics have actually participated in brawls with each other. Some of these incidents are detailed in chapter 7 of this book. On a political level, as noted in chapter 8, Blacks and Hispanics have found themselves in conflict over political control of local school boards. And at the university level, student organizations of Blacks and Latinos find themselves competing for political and economic control, just as in society at large.

One tragic example of the Black/Brown competition for educational crumbs occurred recently at a graduate school in Texas. There, Hispanics dominated a minority student association. For years, however, Blacks and Hispanics had shared leadership roles, resources, and had worked together on areas of mutual concern. The new president of the organization refused to acknowledge Black members of the organization at public functions. Despite attempts by both Hispanic and Black students to resolve the developing differences, the president and some other Hispanics organized a Mexican American student organization, dividing further the institutional resources for, and the influence of, minority students.

Students have related to me anecdotes of similar divisions at other institutions where minority students lobby for the admission of students of their respective minority group at the expense of admissions of members of the other group. Again, minorities find themselves competing for crumbs. If the courts continue along the path of dismantling affirmative action programs, there soon won't be any crumbs left to fight over.

6 ■ Language: Speaking to, and about, One Another

In perhaps no other area of Black/Hispanic conflict is there greater room for cooperation than in the areas of controversy concerning the use of language. Cultural recognition and acceptance cost nothing. Here is the simple bridge over the language chasm: Blacks could learn Spanish; Hispanics could be more tolerant. The language of the New World conquerors could now become a unifying voice of the oppressed. But why should Blacks learn Spanish or even have to tolerate it? As one Black resident of the District of Columbia recently stated: "Anybody can come in this city, speaking any other language but English and get their rights. Black people have been here forever and have no rights. Black people ought to get together and stop this."[1]

It is hard to explain the value and beauty of multilingualism to someone who speaks only English and feels threatened by foreign tongues. While we can prove the value of many things, so far we cannot prove in specific dollar terms the value of speaking more than one language unless a job depends upon it. Of course, neither can we place a monetary worth on many things we find valuable. The lack of quantification does not diminish them. Are we not richer if we can listen to a symphony, attend a play or a movie, participate in a religious service, and leave with some better understanding of the human spirit?

While language is communication, it is much more than that. It is a way of looking at the world. It is an identification with others who share similar cultural values. It is intimate and intense contact with the souls of other humans. Yet the use of language to describe its own essence is inadequate. Let me try to illustrate the pain Hispanics feel when their language is rejected by using some examples I have previously employed.[2] Then, let me try to illustrate how Blacks can be made to feel isolated and excluded when Whites or Hispanics wield language as a method of exclusion.

Try to remember what it felt like to be five or six years old, leaving for school for the very first time. Your name is "Teresita." Your parents are lawful immigrants to the United States. You were born in this country. Your parents and you speak some English, and you are used to hearing that language on television. Spanish is still the primary language spoken in your home, in large part because your grandparents who live with you do not speak English. You are proud of your hard-working, religious family. Yet you feel some anxiety as your mother puts tortillas and lunch meat into a sack for your lunch, walks you to school, and hugs you good-bye.

In the classroom, the teacher speaks English in a very rapid manner. You do not completely understand her. She is calling roll, and all the other kids have Anglo names. When she gets to your name she stumbles over it. She and the other children laugh. Your stomach begins to hurt. "Well, never mind, kids. This name is too hard for me to pronounce," she says. "From now on your name in this class will be 'Teri.' Okay?" She smiles and you don't feel well.

You struggle through the morning's classes. You have always done well at home counting and reading and saying prayers with your mother. But this is different. When the teacher asked the class, "What is 1 plus 1?" your hand is the first to shoot up. "*Dos*," you answer quickly, when the teacher points to you. The other children and the teacher laugh again. At lunchtime you pull the tortillas from your sack. The other children are looking at you. You can't eat.

That afternoon your mother waits for you on the school ground. "How was school?" she asks you in Spanish. You don't want to disappoint her because you know how important she and your father feel it is to do well in school. "It was fine. The teacher gave me a new name. She said my name is now 'Teri.'" Your mother looks at you with an expression you don't understand. Tears fill her eyes, she bends down, looks in your eyes, then hugs you. The rest of the kids are looking at you again.

Now imagine that you are a bilingual construction

worker. You are proud of the work performed by you and your crew. In fact, most of the workers in your unit are people you grew up with in the *barrio* in which you were raised. You socialize with them—Hispanics, Blacks, and Anglos alike—after work, and are generally quite pleased with your job. One day a new foreman is hired. He does not speak Spanish, and orders you and the other workers to quit communicating with each other in what he calls Mexican. When you object he orders you to shut up and speak American. You need the job so you shut up, but you can't help thinking of your high school civics teacher telling you that the slaves couldn't speak to each other in their native tongues either, because the slave owners feared that would lead to rebellion. And you can't help but think of the aging photos of your dad and some of his buddies who were decorated for their service in World War II. Your foreman has no military service record.

Finally, imagine that you are elderly and infirm. One morning upon arising, you feel severe chest pains and numbness in your arms. You reach the phone, and call your doctor, but the office is not yet open. You dial the official emergency number, and in your best English, ask for help. The dispatcher cannot understand you completely because of your accent, and grows impatient. "Please," you repeat. "Help!" You give your address again. As you begin to lose consciousness, you wonder whether an ambulance will be sent, and if so, whether it will reach you in time.

Now imagine that you are an African American worker living in an urban area of the United States. The character of your neighborhood is changing. More and more Hispanics have been moving in. Small stores that used to belong to African Americans and Whites are now owned by Hispanics. Spanish language signs appear in the store windows. Salsa music blares from the windows of your new neighbors.

Your buddies tell you of the difficulties they are having finding jobs. Time after time they approach an employer, only to find "bilingual preferred" listed as a qualification. You took some Spanish in high school but were really not interested in it and don't really remember much of it. But you do remember enough to realize that at your job, some of your co-workers are using Spanish to gossip about your supervisor.

One day your supervisor, who does not speak Spanish, calls you in. "Don't you get tired of hearing Mexican all the time around here?" You shrug. "Well I'm pretty sick of it. Do you know what they're talking about down there?" "Not really, no," you answer. "Well listen. You grew up around here. Don't you think that in this country we all ought to be able to speak English?" You agree. "You're a good man." Several of your co-workers see you leave the office.

The next day your supervisor announces that from now on, only English will be spoken at work. He says he is announcing the rule to maintain safety and because he has received complaints. In order to maintain racial harmony at work, he says, "All employees will be required to speak English only at work."

Your Hispanic co-workers glare at you. When the supervisor leaves, they taunt you quietly in Spanish, then dare you to report them.

"OFFICIAL ENGLISH" EXPLOITATION

These examples highlight the reality that many monolingual people feel threatened by the use of a language they don't understand. This adds to a sense of confrontation between Blacks and Hispanics; most Hispanics speak Spanish and most Blacks do not. When tensions arise between the members of these groups over competition for jobs or in other areas, language difficulties become a flash point.

This confrontation is easily exploited by nativist Whites in the English-only movement. Under the guise of promoting national unity and racial harmony, they urge the adoption of official English laws by the states and federal government, and ultimately in the form of a Constitutional amendment. They would radically alter the legal and social tradition in this country of treating no language as official, just as no religion is treated as an official religion. The English-only movement urges the creation of speak-English-only rules at the workplace, the abolition of bilingual education, and the removal of bilingual ballots. In many instances, they will cynically enlist the help of African Americans who too feel threatened by the presence of the Spanish language. Such has been the case where employers draft minority workers to complain about the use of the Spanish language as the reason for creating a speak-English-only rule in the workplace.

The difficulty with the official English position is that

people who are denied the right to view the world through their language and culture are made to feel inferior and they react negatively. Studies involving bilingual education and broadcasting lead to the conclusion that the rejection of culture and the consequent poor self-image, particularly among children, produce negative feelings that are reflected in a higher educational dropout rate. There is also a higher rate of acting out frustrations in the form of inappropriate behavior. The resentment may be overt and expressed in crime and other antisocial behavior. It may linger covertly at a lower level, producing alcoholism, suicide, or other self-destructive behavior. Or it may simply simmer, breeding resentment and producing the self-fulfilling claim of disloyalty repeatedly thrown by advocates of official-English at those who have some objections to the notion.

In one of the most emotional applications of a variation of an "English-only" rule, a Texas judge in 1995 threatened a Hispanic woman in Amarillo with the removal of her five-year-old daughter after the woman's ex-husband alleged that the mother had not been teaching the child English. In fact, both the mother, Marta Laureano, and her daughter were bilingual. When Ms. Laureano tried to explain that fact to the judge, the judge asked, "So what are you trying to do, make her a maid for the rest of her life?"[3] He ordered her to speak English to the child, implicitly threatening to remove the child from her custody if she didn't, under the theory that the child was being abused by the mother's language use. Hispanic groups nationwide protested the judge's decision. Articles concerning the case appeared in the *New York Times, People* magazine, and international Spanish-language television networks sent crews to Amarillo to carry the story. The judge appointed me as mediator. We were able to work out an agreement between the parents of the child which would rescind the judge's language order. The judge agreed and Ms. Laureano was able to return to the business of raising her child bilingually. The major cause of concern expressed by many who supported the judge's original order was that in this country "Americans" should be able to understand what others are saying, even when that involves a mother speaking to her child. They, and initially the judge, could not understand why a mother's communication with her child should be beyond the control of the state.

While much of the opposition to the use of languages is irrational, Hispanics do need to acknowledge that sometimes the reason monolingual people feel threatened by the use of another language is because the foreign-language speakers are using their tongue specifically to talk about others who don't understand it. Or even if they are not talking about the listeners, they may use the language as a method of exclusion. Whites may complain about being excluded in this fashion, but they as a class have never been the victims of the bitter race discrimination that Blacks have. Hispanics should be particularly sensitive to the fact that Blacks, victims of discrimination at the hands of Whites, might feel justifiably concerned about the uses of discriminatory mechanisms, including language, which could be used to further isolate and discriminate against them.

ACCENTS AND BLACK ENGLISH

Even when Hispanics and Blacks accept and employ English as the preferred method of communication with Whites, they occasionally run into another exclusionary language barrier. Whites claim they cannot understand a Hispanic because of his or her accent. Similarly, they find difficulty communicating with some Blacks because of an identifiable use of Black English. Consciously or subconsciously, some Whites will deny a job, educational opportunities, or other benefits to Blacks or Latinos because of the perception that the minority speaker cannot communicate effectively.

One example of the effective use of this accent barrier is the 1978 decision of the United States District Court for the Southern District of New York in the case of *Mejia v. New York Sheraton Hotel.* The court concluded that the hotel did not violate the civil rights of a Hispanic woman who was denied a position as a front-office cashier. The woman had for a long time effectively performed her duties as a chambermaid. However, when she sought promotion to a visible point of contact with English-speaking customers, the employer balked. Ultimately, the court concluded that the ability to communicate effectively in English was a necessity of the business because the position would necessarily bring the worker in contact and communication with the guests of the hotel. The court claimed that the woman's English-language deficiencies made it difficult to understand what she was saying. In another case, Manuel T. Fragante was denied a position as a clerk with the Honolulu Department of Motor Vehicles because of his Filipino accent, notwith-standing the fact that he had scored first out of 721 appli-cants on the written examination for the job. Fragante sued and at trial proved that the two interviewers who deter-mined not to hire him conducted an informal interview of ten to fifteen minutes. No written interview questions were prepared, and there were no standards, instructions, guide-lines, or criteria for its conduct. There was no validation of questions, and the interviewers were not formally trained in the process. During the trial of his case, Fragante's attor-neys employed a linguist, Dr. Michael Forman, who spe-cializes in interactions between English and Filipino speak-ers. Dr. Forman observed during the trial that attorneys for both sides suffered lapses in grammar and sentence structure, as did the judge. Fragante's English was more nearly perfect in standard grammar and syntax than any other speaker in the courtroom. Fragante testified for two days under the stress of both direct and cross-examination at his trial. The judge and the examiners spoke to him in English and understood his answers. A court reporter understood and took down his words verbatim. Nonethe-less, Fragante lost the case. The court noted that the job he applied for involves dealing with a great number of disgruntled members of the public. It concluded that the position was a high-turnover one where people leave quickly because of the stress involving daily contact with contentious people. The court determined that listeners stopped listening to Filipino accents, resulting in a break-down of communication.

In a few other accent cases, language-minority plaintiffs have had some success. In one case in 1974, a Filipino dental lab assistant won his lawsuit against the University of Oklahoma College of Dentistry. The court found that the employee had been demoted because of his accent. The employer did not prove that the accent interfered with his duties.

Similarly, in other cases, Hispanics have been denied teaching opportunities because White students claim not to be able to understand the speaker. In 1989, the Texas legislature enacted a bill which requires each state institution of higher education to establish a program or short course to assist certain non-native English-speaking faculty to become proficient in English. Across the country various institutions have implemented forms of oral exams and interviews in order to screen out teaching applicants with heavy accents.

In one case, Texas A&M International University in Laredo, Texas, required its prospective graduates, in addition to fulfilling all academic requirements, to take and pass an oral language proficiency exam as a requisite to attaining a bachelor's degree. This public institution of higher education, located near the United States–Mexico border, enrolled a large number of Mexican and Mexican American students. The exam consisted of a student reading a number of sentences into a tape recorder. The student's "oral proficiency" (i.e., accent) would then be evaluated. The sentences clearly sought to identify Hispanic accents. They included:

> The sheep are making the birds cheep.
> The child made a ship of the chip of wood.
> The mother gave a sign of peace as her son ate his peas.

Hispanic students reported feeling humiliated by the experience. As a result, one of my former law students, Joaquin Amaya, and I threatened to file suit on their behalf. The university, in response, abandoned its oral proficiency requirement for graduation in May 1995.

One of the ironies in this entire accent situation is that everyone has an accent. Even the deaf who use sign language to communicate employ identifiable "accented" signs. What is really going on in these cases is that much of the use of accent is a pretext masking race or national-origin discrimination. While no one would question the validity of requiring that our teachers speak clearly enough so that our students can understand them, in many instances it is simply a case of a student not wanting to understand a foreign-looking or a foreign-sounding person. This becomes particularly true when we consider that in our society some accents are considered desirable. People who speak with British or French accents are generally thought to be cultured or sophisticated. People who speak with identifiable Hispanic accents are too often thought to be lazy or uneducated.

I had the good fortune to be raised in the multilingual environment of Santa Fe, New Mexico. Many of my friends and relatives spoke Spanish, English, and even some Native American tongues. Because of its opera and its cultural reputation, Santa Fe attracted visitors from around the world. I grew up hearing different languages, and I also heard English spoken by people with different accents. I was taught that I should show respect for someone who spoke English with an accent; the accent meant that the person spoke more than one language and was therefore educated. Unfortunately, in many quarters, the reverse is now true. We assume that a person who speaks English with an accent, particularly a Hispanic accent, is ignorant.

In the same way, many Blacks suffer discrimination because of the use of an identifiable Black English. This language has its origin in the transactional language of the slaves. Denied the opportunity to use their native tongues and, at the same time, denied an opportunity to learn formal English, slaves developed a Creole language, a variation of which still flourishes. It is used largely in casual conversation and informal talk. One difficulty for Blacks, particularly Black children, is that efforts to instruct children in standard English by teachers who fail to appreciate that the children speak a dialect acceptable in their home and peer community can result in the children becoming ashamed of their language and thus frustrated in their educational efforts in English and in other subjects as well. In a case decided in 1979 by the United States District Court for the Eastern District of Michigan, the Ann Arbor School District Board was ordered to take steps to help teachers at the Martin Luther King, Jr., Elementary School recognize the home language used by their Black students and to use that knowledge in their attempts to teach reading skills and standard English. In its opinion, the court determined that Black children who succeed in their educational endeavors by learning standard English as well as Black English are bilingual. They retain fluency in Black English to maintain status in the community. They become fluent in standard English to succeed in the general society. They achieve this success by learning to "code switch" from one to the other, depending on the circumstances, just as other bilingual children learn to do.

However, not all children learn to make the transition. When they seek employment or other opportunities as adults, it is frequently the case that a White employee will use the identifiable Black English spoken by the applicant as a reason for denying the job. Just like the case with people speaking English with foreign-language accents, Black English becomes the pretext for race discrimination. And, just like the foreign-language accent situation, the person listening to Black English will not understand what he or she does not want to understand. The result, just as for those who speak English with a Hispanic accent, is loss of educational and work opportunities, and a resulting lack of self-esteem.

SHARING OUR LANGUAGES

While Blacks and Latinos struggle with Whites over language and accent issues, we need not turn on each other. For example, when the Dade County, Florida, Commission met in 1993 to consider overturning a requirement that all county business be conducted in English, a number of Black Miami residents attended to speak in favor of keeping the ban on languages other than English. One of them, in reference to the widespread use of the Spanish language, stated, "They are taking over, and I am a victim of that."[4] The Commission overturned the ban, but tension between Hispanics and Blacks was heightened. It doesn't have to be this way.

My suggestion might appear to be an oversimplified solution to some of these difficulties, but Blacks could learn Spanish. Most Blacks outside this country in the Western Hemisphere already speak Spanish or Portuguese. The Spanish language could become a bridge to a New World Afro-Latino identity. Consider, in this vein, the words of W. E. B. DuBois, written in 1919:

It is idiotic for any modern man to be unilingual. . . . Not only are there the usual and obvious arguments of mental and spiritual discipline for a working knowledge of living tongues, but American Negroes must remember that, outside the United States, the overwhelming number of educated people of Negro descent speak French and Spanish. Any effective *rapprochement panafricain* must depend, in the first instance, on the ability of the groups of the Negro race to make themselves mutually understood throughout the world.

But more important than this is the fact that the only white civilization in the world to which color-hatred is not only unknown, but absolutely unintelligible is the so-called Latin, of which France and Spain are leading nations. It is to these nations that we must speak and appeal intelligently and with perfect understanding; with these we must make our closest personal friendships. Today the greatest threat on the earth's horizon is the possible world domination of the "nigger"-hating Anglo-Saxon idea. Only the world union of African, Latin, Asiatic, and possibly Slav and Celt can stop this arrogant tyranny—this death to human aspiration.

Toward all this the first step is language. Every Negro should speak French. Large numbers should speak Spanish and Portuguese. . . .

In every colored community there should be not only French and Spanish classes, but groups reading and speaking, following current newspapers and literature, listening to invited lecturers and visitors, and corresponding regularly with persons in France, Spain, the Islands and South America.[5]

DuBois's words are even more compelling today as we forge a unity among Blacks and Latinos within this country.

Learning another language is not easy. But the increase in the number of Spanish speakers and the explosion and growth of Spanish-language media make the opportunity for contact with the Spanish language very easy for those who want it. Hispanics typically feel great pride in their language and would generally have positive feelings for African Americans who are trying to learn it. In some areas the ability to speak Spanish will greatly improve job opportunities. In Miami, for example, it is now estimated that half of the workforce speaks Spanish. In a 1985 survey by the Strategy Research Corporation, 41 percent of non-Hispanics living in Miami indicated they believe that for their children to succeed, it would be essential for them to read and write Spanish. Sixty percent said they enjoyed socializing with Latino friends. The appreciation of the Spanish language would result in improved individual economic and social possibilities also for African Americans in an increasingly global market. On a broader scale, this opening of communications could improve international relations. The bottom line is that the benefits to learning Spanish would outweigh the difficulties encountered by African Americans.

It would be unrealistic to believe that many Blacks, facing the day-to-day struggle in this country to earn a living and provide for their families, could suddenly become sufficiently interested, and have the time, to learn Spanish. But in urban areas of high concentrations of Blacks and Hispanics, this process could begin. Children are particularly adept at learning languages. Our public schools could become more actively involved with the offering of the Spanish language to those children, Black and White, who demonstrate an interest in it. I have never heard of anyone who regrets having acquired proficiency in Spanish. Accordingly, if a few Black parents acquired some Spanish skills and encouraged their children to do the same, ultimately a momentum may develop that could make at least some level of Spanish acquisition possible on a wider scale in the Black communities.

The other side of the coin is that Hispanics will have to develop a greater sense of tolerance for non-Spanish-speaking Blacks. We should recognize and respect Black English as a legitimate method of communication. Latinos should be willing to encourage African Americans who have an interest in learning Spanish, but they should be tolerant of those who do not. We should be willing, when carrying on a Spanish-language conversation, to switch to English to welcome an African American into the conversation. If we need to return to Spanish because one member of the group does not speak English well, someone in the group should translate for the non-Spanish-speaking African American the nature of the conversation so he or she will not feel excluded.

The first Blacks and Hispanics in the New World communicated with each other in Spanish. It would be ironic if five hundred years later they were not able to do the same.

7 ▪ *Gangs*

When a predominantly White group of boys and young men organize into a cohesive group that dresses alike and uses hand signals to signify membership in the group, they are not called a "gang," they are called Boy Scouts. Of course, Boy Scouts are not organized to commit crimes. Even when White men organize into a group, arm themselves, and openly defy governmental authority, they are still not called a "gang." Rather, they are called "militias" or "Freemen." Gang membership conjures up for Whites the threatening image of young Blacks or Latinos, angry and armed. That menacing image, of course, is exactly the image gang members seek. Yet their hostility is rarely directed against Whites. Instead, when gang violence occurs, it is typically one group of alienated minority youth striking out at another. Latino and Black gang members are killing each other, themselves, and minority bystanders. At the same time, it is in prisons and on the streets, where survival literally depends on forging and maintaining truces and alliances, that some of the most effective steps are being taken to minimize Black and Latino confrontation. There is something we can learn from the uniquely American tragedy of Black and Latino gangs.

WHY GANGS?

Immigrants to the United States often found themselves in a hostile and untrusting environment. Many spoke a different language and held religious beliefs that differed from the majority. To protect themselves, their families, and their cultural identity, immigrants located themselves in communities or in neighborhoods within communities where they could afford mutual insulation against the new pressures of life in America. A need to be accepted and to feel part of something led the younger members of the immigrant community to form protective "gangs."

In the case of Latino immigrants, membership in gangs gave a sense of identity and control in a bitterly racist environment. The gangs were not born out of a desire to engage in criminal activity, although members have clearly committed crimes. Rather, they emerged out of the same need for identification and belonging that is basic to our human nature and which is available in other forums to Whites and wealthy minorities in this country. Fraternity and sorority membership was not an option to impoverished Hispanic youths who were often not even allowed to receive an education. Civic and charitable organizations generally had no interest in attempting to involve minority young men in their programs.

As a result, membership in Latino gangs, particularly in Los Angeles prior to and following World War II, offered a belonging. Members adopted a way of dress and their own dialect not aimed at inspiring criminal activity but at promoting a new Hispanic American identity. The *pachuco* with his outrageous zoot suits and his slowly pronounced language, mixing elements of both Spanish and English, became an icon for oppressed Latinos in Los Angeles. Even today Latino gang members employ the vernacular of the original pachuco. Other young men are referred to as *vatos*. To indicate agreement, a Latino youth may utter, "Simón!" *Ruca* is a crude reference to a girlfriend. These words are neither Spanish nor English. Some English words become pachuco words: "watcha" can mean "watch out." Spanish words acquire a pachuco meaning. *Ahora le* has no Spanish meaning, but involves a wide range of meanings to gang members including approval, as in: "Do you want to do something about it?" The affirmative response, accepting the challenge: "*Ahora le!*" These words are an identity. Even non-Hispanics adopt them in conversations with Latino youths. The language and the dress carry a sense of belonging for Latinos out of the Los Angeles barrios and throughout the American Southwest.

However, the White reaction to the emergence of a unified, proud Hispanic identity has been hostile and swift. The "zoot suit riots" in Los Angeles during World War II were quite simply attacks by United States military personnel on civilian pachucos. A dramatic examination of these themes, vividly exploring the use of language, dress, and culture by Hispanics and the White oppression they endured can be found in the Eddie Olmos film, *Zoot Suit*. It was the violent suppression of these proud people that helped push many otherwise law-abiding teenagers into a more violent, self-protective identity as gang members.

Following the Watts riots in 1965, Blacks began to organize gangs on a scale comparable to those of Hispanics. In the late 1960s Raymond Washington organized a group of kids at Watts Fremont High School into what was to become known as "the Crips." The Crips used blue railroad scarves to hide their face on gang missions. As they began to bully other Blacks, another group on Piru Street in Compton began to use red ones and became known as "the Bloods." In the early 1970s the Crips split into factions, and open warfare erupted among several of them. South-central Los Angeles witnessed continuing clashes between the Crips and the Bloods. Nationwide, local affiliates of the two gangs sprung up. By 1996, a national network of each existed coast to coast.

Young men, Black and Brown, rushed to join gangs for the sake of belonging. They have joined to control even the few blocks in which they live. Many of those gang members, after all, won't leave those blocks for years or perhaps for their entire life. Others joined gangs out of the need to survive. Once a gang is organized and begins to threaten people, the only way to survive is to organize another gang. Poverty, unemployment, and racism have served as the breeding ground. Drugs, money, and sex lure youngsters in the ghettos and barrios into gangs as a way out of their oppression. Gangbangers, and their glorification in the media, offer hope of power to the powerless.

WHY CONFLICT?

By definition, gangs are going to clash. Insults, real or imagined, lead to a cycle of killing and retaliation. By the early 1990s, however, in addition to the tragic yet predictable violence between local gangs, Los Angeles began to witness race-based warfare. The causes and examples are many.

In Los Angeles, Hispanic inmates felt anger watching the outbreak following the first verdict in the Rodney King case. Televised images, shown over and over again, presented the images of Black rioters beating Hispanic men and women along with Whites. By the mid-1990s gang experts identified the emergence of the Mexican Mafia. Hispanic gang members revealed that the Mafia ordered a halt to drive-by shootings among Hispanic gangs and threatened to enforce it with retribution against gang members in jail. Officials feared that the truce enforced among Hispanic members was an attempt to challenge Black gangs for portions of the drug trade. After decades of operating in a live-and-let-live fashion, the result was that Black and Latino gangs became rivals in a power struggle linked to racial conflicts inside the jails and prisons, and to a clash over turf and drugs outside.

In 1993 a retaliatory cycle of bloodshed erupted between two Latino gangs and a Black gang in Venice, California's, Oakwood district, which spread east to the Mar Vista Gardens housing project. Thirteen people died in that year alone.

Demographics play an important role in these confrontations. By the mid-1990s, Hispanic gang membership surpassed Blacks. It is now estimated that there are more than 30,000 Hispanic gang members and approximately 25,000 Black members in Los Angeles. The number of Latino inmates also surpasses the number of Blacks. The result has been an endless cycle of rioting within the jails, gang killings on the streets, and even brawls in high schools in affluent areas.

One jail alone, the Pitchess Detention Center in Los Angeles, witnessed 57 violent disturbances in 1994 and 123 in 1995. The situation there, while more dramatic than in most jails, is typical. Five days of race riots in January 1996 involved 5,300 prisoners. Six guards and 123 inmates were injured following the order by the Mexican Mafia to attack Blacks. These race riots and others like them are often initiated by the tattooed gang leaders known as "shot callers." Hearing rumors of trouble or retaliation on the street, shot callers order attacks on members of rival gangs or racial groups in custody. A ripple of retribution between jail and streets continues, and the potential for open conflict always exists. Even when Latino gangs are targeted by shot callers for retribution by the Mexican Mafia for violating its ban on drive-by shootings or for failing to pay taxes on drug sales, the Latino gangs are required to join their Mafia assailants and attack Blacks when ordered. Blacks, too, are expected to defend other Blacks against the Mafia-ordered attacks.

If the violence were limited to jails and prisons, some might be willing to ignore it. They might conclude that the living hell inmates create for themselves is part of their punishment. But the trouble is that racial gang wars spill out of jails and prisons into the streets and even into high schools. Innocent children, including babies, become victims. Most of those victims are Black or Hispanic.

In Chicago, Black and Hispanic gang members clashed at the David Farragut Career Academy in November 1992. The school, originally all-White, became predominantly Black in the 1970s and then predominantly Hispanic in the 1990s. The problem, according to the principal, Steve Newton, Jr., is that gangs in the area are organized along racial lines. That rift carries over into the school. However, parents and administrators joined in a verbal assault on each other over the race issue. Hispanic gang members, joined by some parents, demanded that Principal Newton, who is Black, resign, and that a Hispanic be named to replace him. The violence and the racial strife spilled from gangs into school and back out again to the neighborhoods.

In Dallas in 1993, Black and Hispanic students fought at several high schools in West Dallas and Oak Cliff. Those battles erupted following the Dallas Cowboys victory parade in downtown Dallas in February 1993, when Black gang members allegedly attacked Whites and Hispanics. The fighting was widely publicized. Soon thereafter, brawls erupted at Sunset High School and at other high schools in the Dallas area. At Pinkston High School in Dallas, a similar battle erupted. Some indicated racial tensions had always been high, but the gang conflict served as the apparent trigger for physical hostilities. In another disturbing incident, more than one hundred students were involved in a racial brawl at Boude Middle School. Kids apparently emulated the example of older gang members, bringing race conflict to the school grounds.

Others have suggested that as long as Whites do not become embroiled in gang violence, society will spend minimal resources in trying to resolve it. But Whites *are* involved. It has been suggested that White guards continue to stir the racial strife within the prisons as a method of controlling inmates and to earn overtime pay when disturbances break out. When these disturbances spill out, the streets and high schools affected are not only those of the impoverished inner cities. In October 1993 and in February 1994, groups of Black and Hispanic students at Palm Springs High School in California battled each other. Racial conflict arrived at the doorsteps of the wealthy, in a struggle one sociologist termed "a fight for who is going to be king of the bottom."[1] As the Palm Springs incidents point out, even wealthy White playlands will not remain immune from the affects of gang violence. In the Los Angeles County jails, where White inmates constitute only 15 percent of the population, White inmates seek to be protected even if it means being locked in higher security areas with less freedom of movement. White inmates find themselves constantly trying to please minority inmates with the hope of currying sufficient favor to be left alone when violence between gangs erupts.

In urban and suburban areas, the fear of gangs and gang violence has led some Whites to overreact. Dress codes have been enacted at malls and in other shopping areas excluding people who wear "gang clothes." Minority youngsters have been removed for wearing pants that are supposedly too baggy or for wearing clothing bearing the insignia of various professional sports teams. The dress codes are enforced selectively against minority members, because of the belief that White youths wearing the identical clothing could not be involved in gangs. When challenged in court, the selective enforcement of these rules has been found to be a violation of the civil rights of the minority youths who were excluded from the mall for no reason other than the wearing of certain clothes. In one incident in Texas, the teenage sons of a Baptist minister were removed from a public fair, for allegedly wearing gang-related clothing. The teenagers, both honor students and athletes, had come with a group of family members directly from a church youth group meeting to the fair. The clothing they were wearing had been purchased for them by their mother. The mother was also an administrator at a local school and responsible for enforcing the school's dress code. Other White youths wearing identical clothing were not detained; the Black young men were detained, photographed, and physically removed from the fair.

In the meantime, gang violence continues. The causes may be local, such as the need to settle a score. They may be territorial. They may be fueled on a regional basis as the number of Hispanics surpasses that of Blacks. Or the causes may be larger and vastly more complex, involving a larger war for control of drug trafficking. Whatever the causes, innocent bystanders, most of them minorities, are falling victim to the conflict alongside the gang participants.

A HOPE FOR RESOLUTION?

As with other areas of Black/Brown conflict, the efforts at conciliation involving gangs receive very little publicity. There have been and continue to be peacemakers. In Los Angeles, community organizations have long sought to bridge the gulf between alienated Latino and Black youngsters. The Watts Community Bridges Project, a component of the Watts/Century Latino organization, has long been engaged in this process. Its projects include taking busloads of Black and Latino students, parents, and ex-gang members on a citywide bus tour beginning at the California Afro-American Museum and ending up among the mariachis and vendor booths on Olvera Street. Many other organizations, including the Multi-Cultural Collaborative in Los Angeles, create an environment where youngsters can speak out face-to-face rather than in the whispers and rumor mills that breed violence. Throughout all of these discussions, one common theme emerges: the improvement in human relations can only occur when there is an improvement in the surrounding social conditions. After all, if our system of capitalism is correct, people will act in their own enlightened self-interest. Human beings will choose peace and prosperity over confrontation and death. But there has to be a realistic opportunity for those who want out of the gangs.

Another theme that emerges from discussions with the peacemakers is that racial tensions are not as heated as the media portrays. Interracial tension is not the sole reason for the unrest. Some neighborhood disputes are unfairly tagged as racially motivated when indeed they are not. Peacemakers also fault the media for the deification of violent, drug-dealing gangbangers. Disaffected and often fatherless young men easily succumb to the images as a way to power and fame.

Even when the gang warfare is overtly and admittedly racial, there is hope for peace between Black and Latino gangs. In early 1995, Blacks and Latinos agreed to form a cease-fire in the Oakwood area in Venice, California, ending two decades of fighting. Their clashes had claimed at least seventeen lives and left more than fifty people injured. Their efforts followed the example of a number of gangs in Los Angeles County. A truce was initially arranged by the Bloods and the Crips in the Watts housing projects following the Rodney King rioting. As a result, gang-related crimes dropped significantly and police presence was reduced. Melvin Hayward, one of the truce organizers, noted, "We are strong in Blackness. We are on the same wave length with the Mexican-Americans. We all could have a stronger alliance if the two races stick together."[2]

Other attempts have been made across the country to help resolve the issue of gang violence. Some have been successful, and others not. In 1993, two hundred gang members from across the United States gathered in Kansas City, Missouri. The major theme of the conference was that economic, political, and social exclusion have pushed disadvantaged people into violence and that this country must offer substantive economic alternatives if the gang problem is to be solved. Participants at the conference included current and former gang members from two dozen American cities. Their gathering, the first National Urban Peace and Justice Summit, focused on extending shaky gang truces. Among the items participants agreed would increase the likelihood of the success of the cease-fire pacts would be to have political and civic leaders focus on urban development, end police brutality, and bring gang leaders into the leadership structure of the communities.

Of course, not all truces are successful. Usually enforcement depends on enforcement by other gang members. Some cities are leery of allowing gang control over truces, particularly where public financing is involved. In the 1960s the City of Chicago found that about one million dollars that were supposed to be used for job training as a way to reduce gang violence ended up funding illegal narcotics and weapons businesses.

Another highly visible failure of peacekeeping efforts among gangs occurred in Minneapolis. In May 1992, four major gangs signed a truce agreement. Police and social service agencies supported the pact. Just four months later, however, a Minneapolis policeman was killed, and gang members participating in the truce were charged with the crime. Even though the truce between gangs remained in effect, the law enforcement community felt that the truce had served to increase the risks to the police while minimizing the risk to gang leaders.

A similar view of a Chicago gang truce was adopted by the gang investigation unit of the Chicago Police Department in October 1992. In that month, gang members agreed to a cease-fire following the death by a sniper's bullet of a seven-year-old boy while he was walking to school. What could be the police objection to a truce? Some viewed it only as a vehicle for division of the city into drug-trafficking areas, free from competition and the resulting gang violence.

One major concern among Whites and Asians is that gang unity and truces between Blacks and Latinos increase the danger of these gangs to other communities. In New York a gang of Hispanic and Black kids from Queens attacked a White family from Utah in a subway station in Manhattan in September 1990. The assailants later indicated they needed money to go dancing. When twenty-two-year-old Brian Watkins defended his parents in the attack, gang members stabbed him to death. Race issues surfaced in New York again, in December 1990, as a result of the assault and rape of a White female jogger in Central Park by a gang of Black and Latino youth. In confessions, two of the gang members described seizing the jogger, striking her with a pipe and rocks, and holding her down while gang members raped her. The jury that convicted them was itself a mosaic: four Blacks, four Whites, three Hispanics, and an Asian.

In the Los Angeles riots following the acquittal of the Rodney King assailants, observers noted that gangs cooperated to destroy more than 90 percent of the Korean-owned businesses in Los Angeles. Close to two thousand such stores were damaged or destroyed. Thus, while to much of White America the riots seemed like random violence, Korean Americans perceived a unified gang reprisal directed against them. One could almost have forecast the pending disaster. During the riots, Mike Davis, a reporter for *The Nation*, was told, "This is for our baby sister. This is for Latasha."[3] The reference was to the death of Latasha Hailius, a Black teenager who was killed by a Korean merchant during an alleged shoplifting incident. The merchant was let off with a $500 fine and some community service. Many within the Black communities had been enraged over the incident. They charged complicity by the White establishment in immunizing Korean merchants from responsibility for similar though less violent acts toward Black customers. Many in the Korean and White communities fear a continuing truce, and the inclusion of Latinos in it, because they are concerned that united Black and Latino gangs spell trouble for Whites and Asians.

Still, the efforts at peacemaking continue. Los Angeles is trying arbitration services to ease tensions. The organization Multi-Racial Americans of Southern California is training racially mixed Black/Latino teenagers in the art of mediation, acknowledging the reality that they are best suited to act as go-betweens in racially tense situations. In Texas, the state's criminal justice system is implementing racial-sensitivity training for inmates at some of its institutions. The hope is that tolerance of people from different racial or ethnic groups, if learned and practiced in prison, can be transferred when the inmate is released. In theory, the result will be a reversal of the typical model whereby racial tensions outside the prison carry inside. Maybe, just maybe, racial tolerance, learned in a life-and-death setting inside a correctional facility, can be carried out onto the streets.

Another possibility for peace lies in the efforts of "OGs" (Original Gangsters). In Los Angeles and in other communities, the efforts of former gang members at arranging truces has been remarkable. Some of them have spent time as gang members in and out of prison, have lost loved ones to gang violence, and now seek to protect their own children from the danger of further harm. Community Build in Los Angeles is one such organization. Weekly meetings include prayers and handshakes. Black and Latino gang members meet and talk to one another in the presence of older former gang members. Truces are arranged and enforced; gang members meet and use their fists in a boxing ring to resolve differences instead of shooting at each other on the streets.

All of these efforts are not going to stop disaffected young men from joining gangs. They will not stop all gang violence. But they do offer hope, to Blacks, Latinos, and Whites alike, that the senseless violence can occasionally be halted. It is time that we learn from these efforts. If largely uneducated and violent gangbangers can understand that it is inappropriate to turn on one another, maybe the rest of us should be listening to them.

8 ▪ *Voting: Coalition or Collision?*

Historical animosities have thus far prevented Blacks and Latinos from being able to maintain effective voting coalitions. In a few urban areas and for brief periods of time, though, minority coalitions have placed their members into elected and appointed positions of power. Blacks and Hispanics will not be able immediately to overcome intergroup rivalries and construct permanent coalitions, but the demographic implications for Black/Brown cooperation in the political arena are staggering. Right now, only one of the ten largest cities in the United States, San Antonio, with a 55 percent Hispanic population, has a single-ethnic group population which constitutes a majority. However, if you combine the numbers of Blacks and Latinos, they now constitute a majority in seven of the ten largest cities in this nation: New York, Los Angeles, Chicago, Houston, Dallas, and San Antonio. Philadelphia contains a combined Black and Latino population of 46 percent. If Asian and Native American populations were added, minorities would constitute an overwhelming majority in these cities.

But Blacks and Hispanics have not yet been able to form a consistent unified voting block. One significant factor is that both the Black and Latino populations are young, with many still below voting age. Further, many Hispanics, as newly arrived residents, have not yet acquired the citizenship necessary to be able to vote. Even though the Constitution of the United States does not require citizenship as a prerequisite to voting, most noncitizen Hispanics find themselves disenfranchised by state requirements of U.S. citizenship for voting purposes. It is up to each state to set the requirements and enforce the mechanics of voter registration, subject to some federal supervision to prevent racial and linguistic discrimination, as noted below in this chapter. In the summer of 1996 the Supreme Court of the United States weakened the power of the states to create congressional districts where minority voters would hold a majority. This precedent, discussed later in this chapter, will likely affect local elections including those for city council positions, school boards, county commissioner races, and other state and local offices. Minority voters will have a harder time electing minority representatives. Finally, perhaps the biggest impediment to Black/Brown political unity is a combination of apathy on the part of individual minority voters and occasional hostility to political candidates of the other minority group.

Despite these obstacles, Black/Hispanic voting coalitions have been successful. They have resulted in the election of minority mayors in New York, Los Angeles, Chicago, Denver, and other cities. These coalitions have tremendous potential for affecting the outcomes of elections throughout the country.

WHO CAN VOTE?

Exercising the right to vote is a power that many now take for granted. However, for Blacks and Latinos the right was only won after terrible struggles.

As previously noted, nothing in the Constitution of the United States limits the right to vote to citizens. Historically, states allowed wealthy immigrants to vote, provided they were White and male. Women citizens were granted suffrage only in this century. Adult citizens of the District of Columbia and territories of the United States still cannot vote for representation in the Congress of the United States. Many have suggested that the real reason that residents of the District of Columbia still cannot elect congressional representatives is that those senators and representatives would likely be Black. After all, the District of Columbia is overwhelmingly Black and the D.C. delegation would thus likely be Democratic. These political realities would make it very difficult to obtain the votes necessary to amend the Constitution of the United States and award these citizens the franchise now afforded to all other U.S. citizens.

Some noncitizens today hold a limited right to vote. The parents of children in the New York City public school system have been able to vote for school board members since 1968. Noncitizen parents of schoolchildren are also eligible to run or to vote for local school councils in Chicago. Tacoma Park, Maryland, allows noncitizen residents a vote in municipal elections. In the early 1990s, the Los Angeles Unified School District took up the issue of allowing noncitizens to vote but came to no conclusion after months of very intense and often bitter debate.

But in order to understand just how difficult it has been for Blacks and Latinos to obtain the right to vote, we need to look back to the time period immediately following the Civil War. Slaves were denied the right to vote. The Fifteenth Amendment to the United States Constitution, ratified in 1870, explicitly eliminated this restriction: "The right of citizens of the United States to vote shall not be denied or abridged by the United States or by any state on account of race, color, or previous condition of servitude. The Congress shall have power to enforce this article by appropriate legislation." In addition to the Constitutional provision, a statute passed by the United States Congress in 1870 provided that "all citizens of the United States who are otherwise qualified to vote at any election by the people in any state . . . shall be entitled and allowed to vote at all such elections, without distinction of race, color, or previous condition of servitude; any constitution, law, custom, usage or regulation of any state . . . , or by or under its authority, to the contrary notwithstanding."

State voting qualifications that discriminated against Blacks could be challenged under the statute and the Fifteenth Amendment, but the litigation process was unrealistically difficult and slow. When a few such suits succeeded, however, the states were quick to create new barriers. Even though they could no longer explicitly deny the right to vote to Blacks on the basis of race or because Blacks had previously been slaves, beginning in the early 1890s a number of states, primarily in the South, enacted new voting qualifications with the purpose of preventing Blacks from voting. Prior to 1890, for example, no Southern state required proof of literacy, nor of the understanding of Constitutional provisions or of the obligations of citizenship, as prerequisites to the exercise of the right to vote. Soon thereafter, these devices sprung up. At the same time, alternative provisions were adopted to assure that illiterate Whites would not be denied the right to vote. The states of Louisiana, North Carolina, and Oklahoma provided that White voters would be exempted from the new literacy tests by a grandfather clause.

While most of these devices were ultimately found by the courts to be unconstitutional, Whites continued to create new barriers just as soon as one was dismantled. For example, in 1915 the Supreme Court of the United States found the Oklahoma grandfather clause to be unconstitutional. The next year, Oklahoma passed another statute requiring all citizens then qualified to vote but who had not voted in the election of 1914 to register within a twelve-day period. Failure to register would result in disenfranchisement. The practical effect of this legislation was to preclude Blacks who had been excluded from voting by the previous unlawful literacy test to be able to exercise the right to vote. As a result, the Supreme Court found the twelve-day registration period to be unlawful.

The battle over voting obstacles continued. Even as late as 1965 the Supreme Court of the United States was called upon to prohibit officials of the state of Louisiana from enforcing Louisiana's "interpretation" test for voter registration. A 1960 provision of the Louisiana state constitution required an applicant to be able to "understand" as well as "give a reasonable interpretation" of any section of the state or federal constitution "when read to him by a registrar." In striking this provision as unconstitutional, the Supreme Court of the United States noted,

> The applicant facing a registrar in Louisiana ... has been compelled to leave his voting fate to that official's uncontrolled power to determine whether the applicant's understanding of the federal or state constitution is satisfactory. As the evidence showed, colored people, even some with the most advanced education and scholarship, were declared by voting registrars with less education to have an unsatisfactory understanding of the Constitution of Louisiana or of the United States. This is not a test, but a trap, sufficient to stop even the most brilliant man on his way to the voting booth. The cherished right of the people in a country like ours to vote cannot be obliterated by the use of laws like this, which leave the voting fate of a citizen to the passing whim or impulse of an individual registrar.[1]

In addition to pursuing relief in the courts, Blacks sought help from Congress. In 1957, the Civil Rights Act of 1957 authorized the attorney general to bring civil actions for injunctive relief to redress denials of the right to vote on account of race or color. Additional legislation was passed in 1960. In 1964, the Civil Rights Act of 1964 provided for the expedition of voting suits. It also prohibited, with respect to registration conducted under state law, for elections held solely or in part for federal offices, the use of literacy tests as a qualification for voting unless they were administered and conducted wholly in writing. Literacy tests had been an effective tool for disenfranchising Hispanic votes as well as Blacks.

Despite these efforts, widespread discrimination continued to occur. After all, state governments had acquired almost two centuries of experience in creating a host of obstacles aimed at denying minority people the right to vote. Minority persons had been required to pay poll taxes, pass literacy tests, give oral interpretations of the Constitution, and pass moral character tests before being allowed to vote. Some states even required a White man to vouch for the character and the morality of a potential minority voter before that person would even be allowed to register. Minority voters, even if registered, were required to sit for several hours answering questions of interpretations of Constitutional law while white voters entered the polling place without molestation. Such discriminatory techniques, together with open intimidation and violence, operated to exclude minorities from participation in voting.

In 1965, however, at the height of civil rights consciousness, protest, and violence, Congress enacted what has been described as possibly the most radical piece of civil rights legislation since Reconstruction. The Voting Rights Act of 1965 sought to prevent minority voting exclusion. It enforces the Fifteenth Amendment's prohibition against the denial of the right to vote by states on the basis of race, color, or previous condition of servitude. As President Lyndon Johnson noted, its purpose is "to eliminate every remaining obstacle to the right and opportunity to vote." The Act created a complex scheme of stringent remedies aimed at the areas where voting discrimination had been most flagrant. Among the remedies was the suspension of literacy tests and similar voting qualifications for a period of five years from the last occurrence of substantial voting discrimination. The Act also authorized appointment of federal poll watchers. It excused those who were made eligible to vote from paying accumulated past poll taxes for state and local elections. It also excused citizens educated in American schools conducted in a foreign language (i.e., in Puerto Rico) from passing English-language literacy tests.

While the Southern states seemed most preoccupied with denying Blacks the right to vote, many Northern states, including the State of New York, had enacted barriers to preclude Puerto Ricans and other Hispanics from voting. The Voting Rights Act of 1965, passed largely as a result of African American struggles, operated to protect Hispanic voters as well. Hispanic legislators joined their African American and White colleagues in its enactment.

In the case of *Katzenbach v. Morgan,* registered voters in New York City challenged the provisions of the Voting Rights Act of 1965 which prohibited the enforcement of the election laws of New York to require an ability to read and write English as a condition of voting. Under the New York laws, many of the several hundred thousand New York City residents who had migrated there from Puerto Rico at the time had been denied the right to vote. The New York voters who brought the suit challenged the federal legislation because it would enable these Hispanic voters the right to vote for the first time. In its 1966 ruling, the Supreme Court upheld the provisions and found that the New York English literacy requirement could not be enforced. From the beginning of the modern civil rights era, then, Blacks and Hispanics were able to work together in order to protect the right of members of each group to vote.

The Voting Rights Act of 1965 was extended in 1970, 1975, and again in 1982. The 1975 extension explicitly broadened coverage to include Native Americans, Asian Americans, Alaskan natives, and those of Spanish heritage. The 1982 extension added new language to Section 2 of the Act. This made it clear that the Act would apply whenever there were discriminatory effects of electoral practices even in the absence of a discriminatory purpose. In 1992 the Act was extended to apply through the year 2007.

As amended, the Voting Rights Act specifically recognizes the difficulties that language-minority citizens face as they seek to exercise their right to vote:

> The Congress finds that voting discrimination against citizens of language minorities is pervasive and national in scope. Such minority citizens are from environments in which the dominant language is other than English. In addition, they have been denied equal educational opportunity by state and local governments, resulting in severe disabilities and continuing illiteracy in the English language. The Congress further finds that, where state and local officials conduct elections only in English, language minority citizens are excluded from participating in the electoral process. In many areas of the country, this exclu-

sion is aggravated by acts of physical, economic, and political intimidation. Congress declares that, in order to enforce the guarantees of the Fourteenth and Fifteenth Amendments to the United States Constitution, it is necessary to eliminate such discrimination by prohibiting English-only elections, and by prescribing other remedial devices.

The Act goes on to prohibit any practice or procedure that is imposed to deny the right of any citizen of the United States to vote because he or she is a member of a language-minority group. Again, while the act is complicated, there are two major provisions that provide a requirement for bilingual voting materials.

First, under what is referred to as Section 4(f)(4), a state or political subdivision subject to the Act must provide any registration or voting notices, forms, instruction, assistance, or other materials or information relating to the electoral process, including ballots, in the language of the applicable language minority group as well as in the English language. (Where the language of the applicable minority group is oral or unwritten or historically unwritten, the state or political subdivision is only required to furnish oral instructions, assistance, or other information.) This provision applies to any state or political subdivision in which (1) over 5 percent of the voting-age citizens were, on November 1, 1972, members of a single-language minority group; (2) registration and election materials were provided only in English on November 1, 1972; and (3) fewer than 50 percent of the voting-age citizens were registered to vote or voted in the 1972 presidential election. Again, while the act and regulations are complicated, states may obtain a judicial determination that they are not covered under these requirements if, during the ten years prior to filing of the action and during the pendency of the action, they can show, in effect, that there has been no application of measures with the effect or intent of abridging the right to vote.

Another section of the Act provides that no state or political subdivision can provide voting materials only in the English language if (1) more than 5 percent of the citizens of voting age of such state or political subdivisions are members of a single-language minority; and (2) that the illiteracy rate of such persons as a group is higher than the national illiteracy rate. Illiteracy, for purposes of this section, means the failure to complete the fifth primary grade.

WHEN IS A MINORITY VOTE NOT REALLY A VOTE?

Even after achieving the ability to vote through litigation and federal legislation, Blacks and Hispanics found their influence to be nonexistent because of the nature of the districts in which they voted. Whites who controlled state legislatures and other governing bodies could very easily draw congressional districts and other election districts to make sure that minority voters always remained a minority within each district. The effect is that minority candidates would lose as a result of block voting by Whites. Ultimately, litigation initiated under the Voting Rights Act resulted in gains in Black and Hispanic representation. Courts that enforced the Act eliminated the "at-large" election system and the drawing of single-member districts with substantial minority populations. How would minority votes otherwise be diluted? Consider first a situation involving a school board. Hispanics and Blacks each constitute 20 percent of the voters. If all five members are elected "at-large" so that the top five vote-getters are the ones who win, and if Whites vote together as a block, there will never be a minority representative on the school board even though minorities constitute a total of 40 percent of the vote. Similarly, even if the school board goes to a system of single-member districts, if Whites draw the districts to make sure that there is not a majority of minority voters within each district, and if Whites vote as a block, there will still never be minority representation on the school board. As a result, minorities who had found an extremely difficult time obtaining the right to vote in the first place would find their vote meaningless without judicial intervention. Federal courts thus intervened. That is the good news.

The bad news is that in 1996, the Supreme Court of the United States, in considering cases arising in Texas and Colorado, overturned state efforts to create legislative districts where minorities would constitute a majority. In Texas, the 1990 census indicated that Texas would be entitled to three additional congressional seats. In an attempt to comply with the Voting Rights Act of 1965, the Texas legislature enacted a redistricting plan. Among other things, the plan created District 30 as a new majority African American district in Dallas County and District 29 as a new majority Hispanic district in Harris County. It reconfigured District 18, adjacent to District 29, as a majority

African American district. The Department of Justice pre-cleared the plan under the Voting Rights Act. However, six Texas voters filed suit alleging that twenty-four of the state's thirty congressional districts, including the three just mentioned, constituted unlawful racial gerrymandering in violation of the Fourteenth Amendment. A three-judge district court held the three districts mentioned above to be unconstitutional. The governor of Texas, George W. Bush, private intervenors, and the United States appealed. On appeal, the Supreme Court of the United States upheld the finding that the districts were unlawful. Responding to the arguments that such districting was necessary in order for minority voters to a have realistic exercise of the franchise, Justice Sandra O'Connor wrote: "Our Fourteenth Amendment jurisprudence evinces a commitment to eliminate unnecessary and excessive governmental use and reinforcement of racial stereotypes." She found, in effect, that the redistricting was "segregation" and therefore unlawful. In one of the more surprising passages of the ruling, Justice O'Connor indicated that she still believes there are cases in which a state could carve out a majority Black or Hispanic district in order to comply with the Voting Rights Act. But the criteria she then set down for establishing such a district are almost impossible to meet.

There are numerous levels of irony in this decision. The state of Texas and others which, after years of employing mechanisms making it difficult for Blacks and Hispanics to vote, affirmatively chose to create districts allowing them to effectively exercise the franchise. The federal government, in the form of the Justice Department, approved the plans. Yet the ultimate branch of review, the Supreme Court, overturned the state efforts to enfranchise Blacks and Hispanics. In North Carolina, African Americans make up almost a quarter of the state's population. North Carolina's White political leaders had deliberately constructed congressional districts to thwart any possibility for a Black representative to be elected in the House. And for more than one hundred years, no Black has been elected to Congress. It was Black and White legislators in North Carolina who banded together with the Bush administration to create new districts that would remedy the diminution of Black political power. But the Supreme Court characterized the efforts as unlawful "political apartheid." The result is that the Voting Rights Act can no longer be used to require the states to create the maximum possible number of congressional districts with Black or Hispanic majority populations.

Nonetheless, some civil rights advocates detect a glimmer of hope. But their hope can be realized only if Blacks and Hispanics work together. It was the late Lee Atwater, then chairman of the Republican National Committee, who formulated the plan to cluster Blacks and Hispanics into a relatively few districts. While that would allow the minority groups to elect representatives who would probably be Democrats, it would also make many of the surrounding seats White and much more winnable for the Republicans. Atwater actively worked with minority leaders and provided the computer software necessary to draw the new districts. His plan succeeded. By 1994, Black representation in the South had increased from five seats to seventeen. At the same time, Republicans had won a majority in the region for the first time since the Civil War. The result was that for the first time in forty years, Republicans captured a majority of seats in 1994 in the House of Representatives. According to some observers, the redistricting accelerated a trend of conservative Whites leaving the Democratic party.

Of course, racial redistricting was only one factor in the resurgence of Republican control of House congressional seats in the South. But one state stands as an example of the results. In Georgia, as a result of the 1990 election, the twelve-member congressional delegation included ten White Democrats, one Black Democrat, and one lone Republican, Newt Gingrich. Following the 1990 census, the state gained an additional seat. After the district lines were redrawn, and the election was held, the result was nine White Republicans, three Black Democrats, and one White Democrat. Blacks gained two seats; the Republicans gained eight.

One of the effects of creating majority-minority districts is to make White politicians less responsive to the needs of minority voters. After all, because the minorities have their own representatives, majority politicians feel little fear of retaliation at the voting booth for failing to respond to the minority community's needs. According to this view, the distribution of minority voters into predominantly White districts may make White politicians more responsive to the minority communities.

Whatever good may ultimately come of this process, there will, in the short term, be fewer minority representatives in the United States House of Representatives and perhaps in local and state offices as well. It will be even more incumbent upon Hispanics and Blacks to work together or run the risk of being a permanently underrepresented minority.

The decision of the Supreme Court in these 1996 Voting Rights Act cases which struck down the minority districts was decided on the slimmest of margins; five Justices voted to strike them and four dissented. The dissenters argued that the Court would regret the day that it had so unnecessarily intervened in the political process. They accused the majority of adopting a double standard that allows gerrymandering for city dwellers, farm dwellers, other ethnic groups including Italians, but not for racial minorities. These racial minorities otherwise, the dissenters noted, would have little chance of ever electing their own to office.

Another result of this decision is that the courts will probably not intervene when Hispanics and Blacks allege that they have been unfairly set at each others' throats in districting. In the early 1990s, Blacks and Latinos separately challenged the districting of the Florida Senate and House. Both alleged that the districting unlawfully diluted the voting strength of Latinos and Blacks in Dade County in violation of the Voting Rights Act of 1965. A federal district court found that the Voting Rights Act had been violated. However, it was unable to create a districting remedy that would accommodate both Blacks and Latinos. The dilemma that faced the court is that it appeared that a remedy for Blacks and a remedy for Latinos would be mutually exclusive. Creating a majority Latino district would dilute Black voting strength. Creation of a Black district would dilute Latinos votes. The court was not certain how to balance the potentially competing interests of the two groups. It acknowledged that in some cases minority interests would be similar and could therefore be aggregated. But it found that there was too much lack of cohesiveness between Hispanics and Blacks to create an aggregated minority district. Hispanics in Florida were made up to a large extent of conservative, Republican Cuban Americans. Blacks consisted of more liberal Democratic voters. The district court determined that no remedy existed for this particular situation. It left the redistricting plan undisturbed, and determined that these "political questions" are best resolved by the legislature.

The Supreme Court of the United States determined, on appeal, that the 1992 state legislative plan did *not* violate the Voting Rights Act of 1965. Thus, the court did not determine how to frame a remedy where competing Latino and Black interests were at stake. Now, as a result of the 1996 Voting Rights pronouncement by the Supreme Court, it is unlikely that courts will ever resolve this dilemma. Many Black and Latino advocates express frustration at a Supreme Court that leaves the state legislatures to work out districting when minorities are underrepresented and at each other's throats politically, but will intervene in the political process and strike down state legislative districting attempts that empower minority voters.

Minority voters watch as the federal courts, which for decades had championed the cause of enfranchising Blacks and Latinos by removing state-imposed obstacles, now effectively disempower those same voters. The immediate solution is for Blacks and Latinos to identify areas of common interest. The wheel does not need to be reinvented. We can learn from the successes and failures of other ad hoc coalitions that have elected minority and White officials sympathetic to the cause of improving civil rights for Blacks and Latinos.

WORKING WITH AND AGAINST EACH OTHER

Not only is New York City the largest city in this country, its demographic breakdown reflects the future of the rest of the country. Blacks constitute 29 percent of the population, and Latinos, growing rapidly, now make up approximately 25 percent of the total. With a 7 percent Asian population as well, minorities outnumber Whites. Despite the potential ability to elect minority representatives and political leaders, the relationship between Hispanic and Black politicians and voters has been inconsistent.

In the 1985 mayoral election in New York City, Ed Koch won handily. He received most of the votes among Whites, Blacks, and Latinos. However, tensions arose that year between Hispanic and Blacks when a coalition of Black politicians endorsed a Black assemblyman from Manhattan, Herman D. Farrell, Jr., for mayor. The expectation had been that Herman Badillo, the former Bronx borough president would receive a coalition endorsement. Farrell was not a unanimous choice among Black candidates. In fact, he received less than 40 percent of their votes, virtually no

White votes, and perhaps one Latino vote in seven. Many Blacks blamed Hispanics for the loss, and many Hispanics resented the lack of Black support for Badillo.

Discussions between Black and Hispanic political leaders following that election resulted in the coalition with White voters that elected African American David Dinkins in 1989. Dinkins challenged White incumbent Ed Koch, with two other White candidates joining in the election. While Dinkins was only able to garner 23 percent of the White vote, Blacks overwhelmingly supported him. More than 93 percent of the Black voters cast their vote for him. The Latino vote was split, but favored Dinkins. Slightly more than 56 percent of the Hispanic voters cast their ballots for him. The result was that Dinkins was elected with 51.1 percent of the overall balloting. Asians cast 99 percent of their ballots for White candidates, representing an even greater percentage than White voters.

In 1993, David N. Dinkins was defeated by Rudolph W. Giuliani. Following the election, many Black politicians suggested that Hispanic officials did not campaign vigorously enough to reelect Dinkins. In reality, though, Giuliani won only one-third of the Hispanic vote, a smaller portion of the Latino vote than that cast for White candidates in Dinkins's successful 1989 race. In politics, however, perception becomes reality. Tensions resulting from that election continued to be felt in the deteriorating relationships between Representative Charles B. Rangel, an African American, and Bronx leaders including Fernando Ferrer and Representative José E. Serrano. This latter conflict centered on the Bronx officials' insistence that their boroughs gain a larger slice of the Federal Empowerment Zone created in upper Manhattan and the South Bronx. Ferrer, the Bronx borough president, had a particular interest in attempting to mend relations. He hoped to be the first Hispanic mayor of New York City.

Blacks and Hispanics began meeting in early 1996 in New York in an attempt to develop strategies for the two groups to work more closely together. Several Hispanic legislators who had boycotted the annual meeting of the Black and Puerto Rican caucus in the state legislature at Albany began to attend the meetings again, indicating they felt the time had come to try to rebuild alliances.

At the same time, H. Carl McCall, the state comptroller and New York State's highest-ranking elected official, indicated his interest in repairing the relationships between Blacks and Hispanics. Many of his colleagues predicted that he would run for a statewide office, perhaps for governor in 1998. Improved relations between Black and Hispanic voters would increase the chances of the election of Ferrer and McCall.

Throughout the country, Black/Latino political coalitions have achieved success in elections, only to find that the maintenance of the coalition is fragile indeed. In Chicago, Blacks and Hispanics worked together to elect Harold Washington as mayor in 1983. By 1990 a new coalition, this time consisting of White and Latinos, put Richard M. Daley into the mayor's office. By 1996, the leadership of the police department and the schools passed from the hands of Blacks and into the hands of Hispanics.

Dallas is demographically similar to New York, Chicago,

and the rest of the nation. Blacks make up nearly 29 percent of the population. A growing Hispanic population constitutes about 23 percent of the total. In the early 1990s, a coalition of Blacks, Hispanics, and concerned Whites were able to place minority representatives on the Dallas City Council, the school board, the Dallas Area Rapid Transit Board, the Dallas County Community College District Board, and several other government bodies. The sometimes fragile coalition expects even more success as the minority population in Dallas becomes the majority. However, setbacks occurred in 1992 over a school board disagreement. After the election of Blacks and Latinos to that body and after two African Americans served as board president, Latinos argued that it was time for a Latino president. When Black trustees refused to support them, Hispanics cut a deal with Anglo trustees. Tensions have simmered since.

In Houston, Hispanic and Black leaders attempted to increase representation among Hispanics on the City Council. The plan, presented in 1991, intended to provide an opening for more Hispanic representation on a body that then had five Black members and one Hispanic out of a total of fourteen seats. The plan was rejected, partly because of overwhelming White opposition. Nonetheless, Blacks and Hispanics worked together in increasing the representation on the school board and on other governmental bodies.

In Washington, D.C., despite recent friction between Hispanics and Blacks, as outlined in chapter 2, political and community leaders are working together to try to resolve tension between the minority groups that constitute a majority of the population.

Throughout the country, other leaders are following these examples. One nationwide attempt was Jesse Jackson's Rainbow Coalition. Although Jackson's presidential aspirations were not successful, many of the coalition's participants gained useful experience in the practicalities of American politics. Their skills may have contributed to later successes in local elections. However, the results of these coalition attempts are and will be mixed, because of the simple fact that members of minority groups do not share a monolithic political ideal. Not all Blacks want to work with Hispanics, and vice versa. There are many points of disagreement, including how to apportion job appointments following election success. It is even difficult to measure the success or failure of these attempts because the statistics following an election may be misleading. We know who won or lost, but we can't really be certain who cast votes for whom. Polls rely on voters' decisions to accurately self-identify as minority group members, and then to accurately report their vote. Neither decision is, nor should it be, mandatory. It may very well be that fewer than 70 percent of voting Hispanics cast their ballots for Mayor Dinkins, but we won't ever know for certain.

THE WHITE VOTE

Black/Hispanic coalitions will succeed in electing and retaining minority candidates only when they are supported by at least a substantial minority of White voters. Failure to include Whites raises the specter that they will seek an alignment with one minority group against another. The reality that Whites will support a minority candidate has been evident since 1966, when Republican Ed Brooke, a Black man, defeated Democratic Endicott Peabody, a White man, to succeed retiring U.S. senator Leverett Saltonstall in Massachusetts. Brooke won 61 percent of the vote. In 1972, Brooke was reelected with 65 percent of the vote against another White candidate. Eventually he was defeated in his 1978 battle against Democrat Paul Tsongas. More than 95 percent of the voters who backed Brooke in 1966 and 1972 were White. In 1992, a Black woman, Carol Moseley-Braun, was elected to the U.S. Senate from Michigan, where roughly 80 percent of the population was White. In 1989, a Black man, Douglas Wilder, was elected governor of Virginia, a state with a 70 percent White population.

In addition, several minority candidates have been elected as mayors of large American cities with a majority White population. Among these are Willie Brown in San Francisco, Tom Bradley in Los Angeles, and Frederico Peña in Denver. Conservative Black Republicans were also successful in attracting White votes in the early 1990s in congressional races. Gary Franks of Connecticut was elected from a district that is 88 percent White, and J. C. Watts of an Oklahoma district that was 83 percent White. Another Black, Colin Powell, drew widespread support among potential White voters as a potential presidential candidate in 1996.

Some Whites, then, will vote for minority candidates. The problem remains how minorities can identify areas of common concern and then how they can most effectively implement strategies that will include the cooperation of Blacks, Latinos, and Whites.

STRATEGIES FOR SUCCESS

The formula for success for Blacks and Latinos in the electoral process involves overcoming self-imposed as well as external obstacles. The first and most obvious step that can be taken to increase minority voting clout is to see that minority people of voting age are registered to vote. In the case of Hispanics, this means that permanent resident aliens will have to become citizens to vote in most elections. Permanent resident aliens who have lived in this country generally for five years or more and who are of good moral character are eligible to become citizens. A number of pro-immigrant groups have begun urging naturalization, that is, the obtaining of citizenship, as a method for more effective participation in American democracy. The Southwest Voter Registration Project and other similar groups have had dramatic success in registering more than one million Hispanics to vote since 1974. Voter registration efforts need to be expanded to include the Black community as well.

Once registered, Blacks and Latinos need to turn out on election day and exercise the franchise. Some have suggested that a feeling of hopelessness contributes to minority voter apathy. Community leaders need to focus on self-determination and motivation to encourage minorities to get out and vote. Even when a coalition candidate is not successful, a substantial turnout for that candidate will tend to make elected officials and future candidates more responsive to the needs of the minority communities.

A third step in the process of increasing Black/Latino voting power is to continue the work of developing and building effective coalitions between the groups. Blacks and Hispanics alike need to become sophisticated in the practicalities of the political process. They will need to negotiate. It may be that in one particular election Hispanics will support a Black candidate for office, and for another office Blacks will support a Hispanic candidate. Both groups need to agree in advance how the coalition will continue to function following an election success. There will need to be lines of communication open in order to defeat the destructive rumors, such as those following the reelection defeat of Mayor David Dinkins of New York in 1993. When a minority candidate is not successful, Blacks and Latinos should examine the hard data to determine what went wrong and change the outcome of the next election. They should examine the data following a victory, to better insure another one.

Another step in the coalition building process is to include concerned Whites. Even in areas with substantial minority votes, or even where race-minority voters constitute a majority, the support of a substantial number of White voters is critical to the election and retention of minority candidates.

One very quick and dramatic way that a Brown/Black voting coalition could increase its strength in a local election would be to have the governing body enact a resolution that would grant noncitizens, many of whom would be Hispanic, the power to vote. This would undoubtedly be a very controversial step, given the long history of White denial of the franchise to Blacks and Latinos, and given the current anti-immigrant sentiment in this country.

Other strategies for success revolve around the issue of single-member districts. Where a school board or another local governing body remains committed to "at-large" elections, Blacks and Latinos should insist, through the courts if necessary, that the representatives be elected from districts. Then they should insist that the districts are drawn so that minorities are not disenfranchised. Notwithstanding the 1996 Supreme Court decision that struck down majority Black and Hispanic congressional districts in Texas and North Carolina, successful court challenges could still be brought where a governing body draws districts to guarantee the disenfranchisement of minority voters.

These and other mechanisms can be used as the building blocks to Black/Brown political coalitions. Creating coalitions will be very difficult in areas like Miami, where studies found not only an absence of coalitional behavior but rather an overt antagonism between Blacks and Latinos. Yet it is in these area where the call for unity is most urgent. In areas where the multiple minority population is small relative to the White population, minority interests should converge out of necessity. Where it is large, it should converge out of the realistic hope of wielding power.

Finally, one other strategy may be useful in Black/Brown coalition building attempts, and in the attempt to elect more minority candidates to office. That approach would co-opt the notion of cumulative voting from American corporate law where it has long worked very well to insure the representation on the board of directors of those who hold less than a majority of the shares.

The process is actually very simple. A voter can cast as many votes as there are positions up for election. A voter may cast all of his or her votes for a single candidate. That is, voters can "cumulate" votes. Here is an example. Assume that there is an eight-member school board. All the board seats come up for election. Assume that within this district Black voters constitute 15 percent of the voters. Under the traditional approach, in an "at large" election, Black voters would never be able to elect a board member if Whites voted together as a block. Every time a seat became vacant, and assuming racial-block voting, the Black candidates would lose on an 85–15 percent vote. If the school board were to break the eight-member board into single-member districts, we could have the same problems discussed earlier. That is, either the single-member districts would be broken down so that Black voters continued to be a minority in each district and unable to elect a director, or the district would be divided along racial lines, in which case the Supreme Court of the United States might strike them as unconstitutional. However, under cumulative voting, there is a solution. Each voter in the district would have eight votes. Each voter could cast the eight votes in any way he or she saw fit. If there were one Black candidate for office, a Black voter could cast all eight votes for that one candidate. If all other Black voters did the same thing, that Black candidate would be elected due to a mathematical formula that guarantees that with an eight-member board, 12 percent of the voting-age population could elect one director if they all cumulated their votes. Whites could not cumulate their votes to prevent the election of this one official. For years this system has allowed minority shareholders in corporations (minority in terms of the number of shares they held) to pile all of their votes on one or more candidates. As a result, a substantial minority block of shares is able to elect one or more members of the board of directors of a corporation. The same principle could apply to political elections.

The criticism of cumulative voting is that in most federal elections, implementation of cumulative voting would require an amendment to the Constitution of the United States. (It would not be a problem in state and local elections.) Another problem often raised is that cumulative voting is too complicated. The implicit argument is that minority voters are simply not sophisticated enough to understand or implement it. I suspect the opposite is true; it would be very simple for Black and minority voters to understand that they could cast all of their votes for a minority candidate. It is also not too difficult for Black and Hispanic coalitions to determine how to vote cumulatively to elect more than one member of a local board by distributing the votes among more than one candidate. The difficulty for many White voters is that this method would guarantee minority representation. It could accomplish this minority representation without running afoul of the recent Supreme Court pronouncement that precludes the creation of minority-majority districts.[2]

I am certainly not the first to urge the use of cumulative voting to allow minorities more equitable political access. Lani Guinier, a law professor who was nominated by President Clinton to serve as a high-ranking official within the Justice Department was ultimately denied the appointment after publicity surfaced regarding her writings on this topic. She was denounced as urging the granting of more than one vote to minorities. In reality, her approach may have represented too much of a threat to those who realized her ideas would work; Hispanics and Blacks would be empowered in proportion relative to their numbers in the population, rather than continue to be invisible in elective offices.

The initial success of cumulative voting and the other strategies outlined here depend on the willingness of competent and committed Black and Latino citizens to take the initiative and exercise the leadership necessary to seek and effectively hold public office. Their continuing success depends upon these newly elected officials being able to demonstrate their ability to serve not only their minority constituents, but the rest of America as well.

9 ■ *Bringing Us Together*

Throughout this book we have examined areas of conflict and cooperation among African Americans and Hispanics. The successes and failures of efforts at fence mending offer us crucial lessons. Before America becomes hopelessly Balkanized in an endless cycle of racial resentments and recriminations, we simply must forge alliances and stress commonalities, not differences.

Some cynical Whites, with the implicit support of disenfranchised Latinos and Blacks, are pitting minority groups against one another in debates over immigration control, language rights, welfare reform, and affirmative action. Their view of America is an endless "the Good, the Bad, and the Ugly" scenario, with Blacks being enlisted to oppress Latinos and Latinos being enlisted to oppress Blacks, all on behalf, ultimately, of White bigots. Looking at the demographics, White supremacists realize that their worst fears will soon come true. They will lose their status as the majority within their lifetimes. In this democracy, they cannot count on an institutionalized system of apartheid that enabled minority Whites to remain in power in South Africa until its system collapsed. Their only alternative, and a potentially very effective one, is to foment racial antagonisms between the two largest minority groups.

Most Whites do not hold this extremist position. However, according to a 1994 Harris survey, neither do most Whites believe that racial discrimination by Whites against Blacks and Hispanics still exists. Since they do not believe that Latinos and Blacks are the victims of White discrimination, any efforts at affirmative action or bilingual accommodation is viewed as reverse discrimination against Whites. Conflict between Blacks and Hispanics is seen as a struggle for jobs, educational opportunities, and other things that belong to Whites in the first place. Accordingly, unless the conflict directly involves them, most Whites up to this point have shown little interest in assisting peacemaking efforts between Blacks and Latinos.

Unfortunately, some leaders of both minority groups have been all too willing to join in the fray. A national Hispanic leader was quoted in the *Washington Post* as stating, "Hispanics feel like they have been dealt out of the political system, that it takes care of Blacks but not Hispanics." The *Dallas Morning News* quotes a Black school administrator and a former school board member as indicating during a staff training session that Hispanics tolerate incompetence. She then wondered whether it is a "cultural trait" of Hispanics. Other less-sophisticated Hispanics and

Blacks employ White racist slurs against the other group. The result is resentment, retaliation, and the potential for violence. No society can thrive and prosper under those conditions. A resolution will only occur through the active self-determination of Blacks and Latinos, and the cooperation of a substantial number of fair-minded Whites.

SELF-DETERMINATION

For years many Whites have played the "blame the victim" game in race relations. They have suggested that the reason that Blacks and Hispanics suffer higher unemployment and lower education rates is through their own lack of initiative, ability, and efforts. This view is, of course, untrue. It is a stinging slap in the face from those who have created and perpetuated a system that denies many minorities even the basics, and then mocks them for their poverty and feelings of hopelessness. Nonetheless, it can serve as a wake-up call. Minorities have always had to work harder to be successful than Whites in this country. We don't have to wait for White approval, support, and encouragement to improve ourselves, our communities, and our relations with one another. We can begin to overcome the hatred, resentment, and bigotry by standing up for ourselves and each other and by enlisting the support of well-intentioned Whites in the process. It is not going to be an easy matter, nor is it going to be painless. Our efforts at building bridges will be resented by many, and dismissed as naive by many within our own communities. Without them, though, we play the game of submergence: while we push each other down, the bigots remain on top.

At the same time we must avoid the temptation to blame all Black/Latino conflict on Whites. That approach only allows the conflict to continue by absolving Blacks and Latinos from any responsibility for it. One scholar, for example, has asserted, "When a Vietnamese family is driven out of its home in a project by African American youth, that is White supremacy. When a Korean store owner shoots an African American teenager in the back of the head, that is White supremacy."[1] I would respectfully disagree. Both of these acts are criminal acts perpetuated by minority people who should be held personally responsible for their actions. Asserting that "White supremacy" is to blame places a great deal of power in the hands of the White supremacist. Ironically, it serves the interests of White supremacy to suggest that minority people are so gullible that they can be led into criminal acts against each other by the will of Whites. I think Blacks and Hispanics are stronger than that. I think that they can and must act responsibly toward one another, regardless of whether some Whites would like to see them at each other's throats.

At the beginning of this book I urged that we speak bluntly if we ever hope to resolve our differences. I take the same approach now. Here, then, are some of the approaches we can take in the process of beginning Black/Latino cooperation.

1. Acknowledge Our Own Non-White Identities

Hispanics play into a White supremacy model when they claim to be White and therefore implicitly better than

Blacks or other dark-skinned Hispanics. I recall growing up in northern New Mexico, where some Hispanic people vehemently denied having any Mexican or Indian blood. Rather, they insisted that they were "Spanish." On the walls of their homes were the coats of arms of the Spanish conquistadores. Yet very few women made the journey from Spain to the New World. Of those that did arrive, fewer still journeyed from what is now Mexico northward into what is now New Mexico. By the 1900s, four hundred years had passed since the arrival of the Spaniards. In that time, there clearly was a great deal of "intermarriage" involving Spaniards and the indigenous peoples. The racial caste system discussed in chapter 2 reflects this reality. The pure "Spanish" identity claimed by some Hispanics obviously involved more than a genealogical inaccuracy. For some, it represented an attempt to distance themselves from the lower socioeconomic Hispanics and Native Americans among whom they lived. They had accepted the White notion that darker-skinned and indigenous people were inferior to Europeans. Similarly, within the Black community, there have historically been tensions between fairer-skinned and darker-skinned African Americans.

More recently, friction between newly arrived Caribbean peoples and African Americans has become a growing phenomenon. Realizing that Black Americans suffer tremendous discrimination, some Caribbean immigrants will deny that they are Black, though most White Americans would consider them to be Black. American Blacks resent that some of these folks insist on being characterized as Hispanic rather than Black. At the same time, some of the

Caribbean arrivals find much more cultural and linguistic kinship with Hispanics than with Blacks. They resent being lumped into the category of African American because they feel they will have a more difficult time being accepted by Whites.

All of these instances play into the hands of a simple, destructive model that has plagued this country for generations: White is good and dark is bad. Trying to identify with the oppressor rather than help alleviate the oppression doesn't work. Many Whites will still identify a Hispanic, a Caribbean person, or a fair-skinned Black American as a minority and treat him or her accordingly. Even many Whites who harbor little prejudice will nonetheless identify a minority person by skin color, even if they like or love that person. Consider, for example, the situation involving some of the grandchildren of the former president of the United States, George Bush. President Bush certainly is no racist. His son Jeb is married to a Hispanic woman. In a well-publicized event, the former president, in response to questions by the media, pointed to his grandchildren and said, "They're the little Brown ones." President Bush no doubt loves his grandchildren and intended no disrespect for them or his daughter-in-law in his characterization. However, he identified them by what he, and most likely most White Americans, would consider their primary characteristic, their darker skin color. After all, how often have you heard White people describe others this way? The only reason, in any event, that these children or other Hispanics would claim a White identity would be to elevate their status over darker-skinned Americans. This raises questions relating to the "perception vs. self-identification" dilemma noted in chapter 3. Are we Brown or Black because White America says we are? Or are we Brown or Black because we say so? If we say we are not Black or Latino, and Whites say we are, what are we? Why should White America be the standard bearer?

At some point, Whites may no longer define non-Whites based on race or color. Until that time, however, Hispanics must demonstrate solidarity with Blacks by embracing a non-White identity. Our blood is intermingled. Hispanics and Blacks are not even mutually exclusive groups. We should be proud of who we are and proud to stand together, though we are also distinct, against a White society that defines us in simplistic monolithic terms.

2. Acknowledge the Harm Each Group Has Suffered

It is destructive for Blacks and Hispanics to engage in the game of claiming that one group or the other has suffered more at the hands of Whites, or that one group has received greater benefits from civil rights laws than another. Each group must recognize the pain that the other has suffered from Whites and, most recently, from each other. The ancestors of today's African Americans were brought in chains from Africa. Many more perished on the journey than survived to live in bondage. Their families were destroyed. They were treated worse than animals. They were denied education and basic dignity as human beings.

Most modern Hispanic immigrants came to this country voluntarily. However, in many instances they did so to escape starvation and brutalization. Some were fleeing corrupt regimes that have been supported and backed by the United States. The ancestors of many Hispanics have suffered a brutal and demeaning history. They too have been denied the educational and work opportunities afforded to Whites. They have fought in the nation's military service in proportionately greater numbers than Whites, only to be called un-American because of their justifiable pride in their language and culture. Even today, many Hispanic migrant workers are forced to live under conditions resembling slavery. They work in dangerous conditions, often without basic necessities such as toilets and clean drinking water. They move from locale to locale harvesting crops and, as a result, their children receive little education.

Recently, Blacks and Hispanics have sometimes played the role of each other's oppressor. It is time for this cycle to stop. Each group has suffered pain at the hands of Whites and from each other. Each group will suffer even more if the cycle continues. One way to become aware of the history of each group is to participate formally and informally in an educational process. Although dwindling in number and support, many institutions of higher learning continue to offer Black studies and Hispanic studies courses. On a less formal level, Hispanics should attend functions devoted to Black history. For example, in Texas each June 19, African Americans celebrate that date in 1865 when news of the emancipation finally reached Texas. Celebrations are held throughout the state. Unfortunately, few Hispanics attend. Similarly, Mexican Americans celebrate the 16th of

September each year. That commemorates the date in 1810 when Mexico began its drive for independence from Spain. In the early morning hours of September 16 of that year, a Catholic priest, Father Miguel Hidalgo, who was one of the conspirators in a plot to gain independence for Mexico from Spain, ran to his church and rang his bells in the middle of the night to awaken his parishioners to the struggle for independence for Mexico. The result of Mexican independence from Spain was that ultimately the American Southwest became part of the United States. Few blacks attend 16th of September celebrations.

There are numerous other opportunities for Blacks and Hispanics to participate in and appreciate each other's culture. Black History month celebrations each February offer Hispanics an opportunity to begin to appreciate Black contributions. "Cinco de Mayo" celebrations, commemorating the Mexican army's victory over a French invading force at the Battle of Puebla in 1862, are held throughout the Southwest. In Miami, New York, and other cities, celebrations of Hispanic and Black culture offer opportunities for contact on a human, friendly basis in a relaxed setting. Merely attending each other's festivals is clearly not going to solve Black/Latino conflict, but it can be one of many first steps toward reacquainting themselves. We don't need White permission or encouragement to continue the process of understanding each other's history and the history of this country. A mutual appreciation of who we are can only assist in the process of forming alliances. Each group needs to become aware of the tremendous contributions that the other has made to this country. Each needs to become aware of the tremendous pain the other has endured in the process.

3. Educate Ourselves

The key to success in this country is education. We must make every sacrifice to afford that opportunity to ourselves and to our children. If the courts close off the more prestigious institutions to us, we must take advantage of community college systems, and state university systems. We must work very hard and do very well at that level in order to have a greater shot at prestigious graduate education programs later. If our interest is in technical fields, we must seek out the best vocational and technical training programs available.

Then, having achieved an education, we need to use that education not only to better ourselves and our families but to better our communities. When I was a law student at the University of New Mexico School of Law in the early 1970s, one of my law professors, Cruz Reynoso, told us that for some reason we had been given more opportunities than others from our communities. We had achieved the privilege of a higher education. As a result, he told us, we had an obligation to give back to our community. He told us that our first obligation is to be the best students we can be. But beyond that, we had further obligations. If we found that in the course of our day, after we worked, studied, and took care of our families, that we had no time left to give back to our community, the solution to the dilemma was simple: we must set our alarm clocks an hour earlier. His words can serve as an example for all of us. We have got to educate ourselves and carve out time to use that education to improve our communities.

Professor Reynoso's words echo "The Talented Tenth" suggestion of W. E. B. Du Bois. His view, later refined, was that Blacks needed to develop an educated leadership consisting of physicians, lawyers, technicians, business people, teachers, and social workers committed not only to themselves but to their communities. These people would be committed to the notion that their private profit did not substitute for the public's welfare. Rather, they would strive to display a selflessness and a dedication that would encourage others to join them in a common struggle for the improvement of the Black condition.[2] The words of DuBois apply to all of us as we seek to strengthen our communities.

Specifically, we must produce attorneys who are willing to take the tremendous guarantees written into our Constitution and our laws, dust off the books, and make the courts apply those principles to better the lives of our communities. The laws are meaningless without lawyers willing to use them and without litigants willing to step forward and challenge those who insist on engaging in unlawful, race-based discrimination.

Those who receive an education in the business field need to use their education to build an economic infrastructure that will help support people from our communities. Those who choose health care have to work to insure that the care is available to everyone and not just those who can afford it. In every other professional and technical field, our trained and educated young people have to carry the commitment back to their homes and their communities. We need the support of Whites in this endeavor but we do not need their permission.

4. Build Effective Coalitions

We need leaders in the effort to build effective coalitions. Unfortunately, "high status" Blacks and Hispanics currently seem the least enthused about minority coalitions. Many have acquired their slice of the pie and see little interest in helping others do the same. At the same time, a 1994 Harris poll indicated that there is considerable contact in all settings between Blacks and Hispanics. A large number report they are willing to work together to solve problems that confront us all: drugs, poor educational facilities, homelessness, inadequate child care. Our leaders must be willing to put aside self-interest and involve themselves in the work of building coalitions that many in both communities would like to have. We cannot afford to have affluent Blacks and Latinos turn their backs on the work of improving the lives of their own peoples. We desperately need their leadership.

Even as we wait for leaders to emerge to assist on a national or regional basis, there are many informal coalition building activities in which we can engage. Neighbors can get to know one another. Parents can work together in the schools. Simple acts of kindness can form the basis for cooperation in later struggles. Parents can become actively involved in peacemaking efforts in the schools. Blacks can contribute to scholarship-raising activities by Hispanics and vice versa. Every act of racial tension between Blacks and Latinos can be countered by a hundred acts of individual kindness. Where racial strife occurs, outpourings of cooperation must follow, as it has in school systems in Dallas, Palm Springs and other communities following trouble between minority students. When violence surfaces, active peacemaking must follow, as it has in Los Angeles following gang disturbances. Every incident of tension between our communities must become an opportunity for building greater tolerance and cooperation. Blacks and Latinos should join each other's civic and civil rights organizations. Latino student organizations should openly encourage Black participation and vice versa. Coalitions can develop on a neighbor-to-neighbor, block-to-block, school-to-school basis.

To give direction to local coalitions, and to speed their development, we must convene a national Black/Latino summit. Business people, political and religious leaders, educators, teachers, blue-collar workers, housewives, parents, and students should gather to discuss the areas of concern noted throughout this book. Workshops could focus on identifying problem areas and developing strategies to confront them. The results and resolutions of this national summit would be carried back to local coalitions for implementation. The event could become an annual meeting. Existing Black and Latino civil rights organizations could take the initiative and create the first such conference.

5. Increase Economic Opportunities for One Another

The number of Hispanic-owned businesses has increased dramatically in recent years; the Census Bureau reports a 76 percent increase between 1987 and 1992. The Commerce Department estimated that 863,000 such businesses existed in 1992. The president of the United States Hispanic Chamber of Commerce estimated that the number would reach two million by the year 2000. In July 1996, Evert Ehrlich, Under Secretary of Commerce for Economic Affairs, indicated that a "vibrant, Hispanic sector is growing in America." The number of black-owned businesses is also on the increase in this country. In 1992, African Americans owned 621,000 businesses, representing a 46 percent increase over the preceding five years. The net effect is that Hispanic business people and Black business people are increasingly in the position to contribute to the economic well-being of their families and friends. As a further step in improving relations between Blacks and Latinos, each should also be willing to hire qualified members of the other group.

This notion is not just a matter of justice; it is also a matter of good business sense. Increasing the number of Black employees in a Hispanic firm will undoubtedly make that firm more appealing to Black customers and clients. The same is true of a Black-owned business which places Hispanics in positions of high visibility. Hispanic and Black businesses can engage in joint ventures of mutual interest and benefit. Besides creating additional employment opportunities for minority workers, this strategy will help prevent the conflict that occurs when merchants are perceived as taking money out of a community without giving back to it. The situation involving Korean/Black strife in Los Angeles stands as an example.

Alliances of Black and Hispanic business people, in addition to increasing domestic marketing opportunities, stand a much better chance of reaching a global market. In this regard, minority business people may even have some advantages over their White competitors. Black and Hispanic firms can use the language and cultural ties of American Hispanics in marketing to Latin America. White firms already do so, sometimes well, or sometimes with disastrous effects. When Chevrolet marketed its "Nova" in Latin America, it failed to realize that in Spanish "no va" means "it doesn't go." Black/Hispanic firms might have better results, perhaps even representing predominantly White businesses. Black/Latino firms can use the racial identity and cultural ties of Black Americans in marketing tourism, food products, clothing, and other products to Africa and the Caribbean. These same firms can utilize the talents and resources of Asian and White Americans in forging additional economic and business alliances to market worldwide. Former Secretary of Commerce Ron Brown was actively involved in this process until his untimely death in 1996.

While the majority of Black- and Hispanic-owned businesses are small businesses, there is no reason why talented individuals in these firms cannot begin to think in terms beyond "Ma and Pa" operations. While we might be able to survive by selling products and services locally, we can thrive by selling products and services nationally and internationally. Just as with the professions, the ability to engage successfully in business does not intrinsically reside in the White or Korean population to any greater extent than in the Black and Latino.

Hispanics and Blacks must work together to assist in the process of obtaining capital for these ventures. Many banks and financial institutions will not even discuss a loan for start-up capital for small businesses. One important source is the Small Business Administration (SBA), which guarantees loans. In 1994, the SBA approved loans in the amount of 431 million dollars for Hispanic-owned businesses and 202 million dollars for Black-owned businesses, less than 5 percent and 2 percent respectively of the total amount of approved SBA loans. Hispanics and Blacks must lobby together to insure the availability of funding under these programs. After all, according to the 1996 policy summary of the national Hispanic Leadership Agenda, the majority of Hispanic businesses on the Hispanic business magazine list of the five hundred largest companies started their businesses with less than $50,000. At the appropriate time, and with appropriate resources, Blacks and Hispanics should consider creating banks and financial institutions to serve their communities and to assist in the provision of start-up capital for new minority-owned businesses.

6. Avoid Repeating the Sins of White America

Blacks and Hispanics have long been the victims of racism and oppression in this country at the hands of Whites. We cannot afford, as our economic and political strength grows, to imitate the oppressors. Members of both groups should consciously strive to avoid the racist exclusion or oppression of each other or of Whites. We should remain committed to an ideal of integration as the appropriate moral vehicle for building a just society. We must be better than our tormentors. We must stand willing to resist racism in all of its forms and in all of its venues. At the same time, we must be willing to extend a hand to each other, to other minority people, and to sympathetic White people in an attempt to create a more just America.

7. Stick up for Each Other

In this regard, we must be willing to act as each other's big brothers and big sisters. When we witness an example of unfair treatment directed at a Black or Hispanic person, we must be willing, at a minimum, to say clearly, honestly, and openly, "That is wrong." This is often an extremely difficult and painful thing to do, particularly when we ourselves will face retaliation for it. But our silence in the face of oppression makes us an equal party to it. Standing up to a bully, with the support of others, is the most effective way to stop the bullying. Silence breeds complicity.

Sticking up for one another means not only objecting when White people mistreat other minorities. It also means taking a stand when Blacks degrade Hispanics and vice versa. A very simple and polite, "I don't think you should do that" or "I don't think you should say that" can effectively let, even those we love, know that we disapprove of their words or conduct. If they think anything of us at all, they may change their behavior. Even if they don't change their behavior, they will not have the mistaken idea that they are acting for anyone other than themselves. These small yet courageous acts can go a long way toward reducing tensions between Blacks and Hispanics. Even when they do not immediately stop the misconduct, objecting to the behavior lets the Black or Hispanic victim know that not all Blacks feel bad things toward Hispanics and vice versa.

8. Enlist the Support of Committed Whites

Whites are a majority in this country. Even in the next century, they will constitute a plurality. For the immediate future they will hold economic and political power in disproportion to their numbers. Some of them understand, as Barry Switzer, coach of the Dallas Cowboys, once put it, "Some people are born on third base and go through life thinking they hit a triple." We must help to educate Whites about their history and ours. White Americans need to realize that the economic and political strength they hold was, to a large extent, built on the backs of minority people in this country. Black slaves built the economic base of the South. Hispanic workers have done the same in forging the agricultural strength of companies and service industries throughout the Southwest. Chinese workers laid the railroads. America stole the very lands that now constitute the productive heartlands of America from the Native Americans.

This racism was institutionalized in our very structure.

Language opposing slavery, for example, was omitted from early drafts of the Declaration of Independence. The original Constitution of the United States institutionalized and perpetuated slavery. Article One, Section 9, Clause 1 of the Constitution of the United States provides that "the migration or importation of such persons as any of the states now existing shall think proper to permit, shall not be prohibited by the Congress prior to the year 1808." This clause represents a political agreement by the framers of the Constitution to protect the slave trade at least through the year 1808. Many of the individuals upon whose achievements the success of the American Revolution depended were slave owners, among them George Washington and Thomas Jefferson. Some British leaders at the time of the American Revolution noted the irony that the ringing calls for liberty and inalienable rights of human beings were being proclaimed by men who claimed the right to own other men. This is not to detract from the tremendous framework for freedom and democracy that was established as a result of the efforts of these and other individuals. It is not to detract from a Constitution and system of laws that provide more freedom than any other country in the world. The success of the American experiment can be seen in the fact that people vote with their feet. This country admits more legal immigrants, and receives more illegal immigrants each year, than any other country in the world. People don't come here because they like our weather; they come here for the opportunities of economic and political freedom that are lacking in their homelands.

Fair-minded Whites will recognize the need to include

Blacks and Hispanics in the American dream. They will recognize the need to refrain from the race baiting that can only result in the destruction of the society to which we all owe such a great deal. They may be literally caught in a crossfire by fomenting Black/Latino conflict.

We cannot allow Whites to roll back the modest gains made by minorities under the rationale that discrimination is a thing of the past. Legalized or *de jure* discrimination may have passed but its effects linger. The statistics including educational achievements, earning levels, and dropout rates for minorities together with other indices contain a damning portrait of the lingering effects of racism. Professor Stephanie Wildman identifies a broad, insidious, and ultimately extremely powerful White privilege that undermines the attempts by the legal system to remedy these effects in her 1996 book, *Privilege Revealed: How Invisible Preference Undermines America.*

We can also not let go unchallenged the notion of some Whites that runs like this: "I haven't discriminated against any minorities. Therefore, they shouldn't have a chance through affirmative action to a slot in school or a job that excludes me." The mothers, fathers, and ancestors of these Whites have been afforded many more opportunities than those of their minority counterparts. These Whites have undoubtedly benefited from this. Only within our lifetimes have the public schools been integrated. It has only been in the last four decades that strides were taken to enfranchise minority voters. It has only been since 1964 that federal legislation guaranteed workers the right to be free from racial discrimination in employment decisions. Only in

1967 were state laws precluding Blacks and Whites from marrying each other stricken as unconstitutional.

Similarly, we must help educate Whites to the reality that some speech directed by some Whites at minorities has a damning effect particularly upon minority children. When White people speak demeaningly on a racial basis toward minority people, it reenforces a White supremacy model that breeds resentment and rebellion. The belief that some of this speech is protected by the First Amendment is no moral defense. We would be acting within our rights under the First Amendment to tell people that they are fat and that their spouse is having an affair, but good manners would dictate that we would not exercise that right even if the comments were true. We would refuse to make the comments out of respect for the feelings of the listener. Or if nothing else, we might decline to make the comments because it would make us appear boorish. We must help Whites understand that hateful speech, even when legally protected, makes them look boorish to us and to other educated Whites. They may not care. But at least we have indicated that we will not remain silent in the face of their misconduct.

9. As We Work toward Unity, We Must Project Unity

The media's focus on Black and Hispanic relations is predominantly negative. Headlines scream "Growing Rift Tatters Nation's Ethnic Tapestry," "Don't Ignore Black/Hispanic Tensions," "Problems between Blacks and Hispanics Likely to Grow in the Foreseeable Future" and on and on. But is the tension between some Blacks and some Hispanics really as pronounced as the media would have America believe? When an interracial couple gets into a public argument, it does not necessarily mean that the squabble is over race. The argument might concern family finances, differences on child rearing, jealousies, or any other number of topics. Similarly, a dispute between Blacks and Hispanics does not necessarily involve elements of race. Race tensions can come into play when Blacks or Hispanics are goaded into making racially derogatory comments about the other group. Certainly, racial conflict sells more newspapers than racial cooperation does. No greater example of this exists than in New York or Los Angeles, where millions of Blacks and Latinos get along every day. But only one dispute can make either city appear to be a racial cauldron. We do not need to play into the hands of headline writers by translating what otherwise might be simple human disagreements into race issues. We can voluntarily refrain from giving the soundbites that sell our dignity and self-respect along with newspapers.

Similarly, when there is evidence of Black and Hispanic cooperation, we must make every effort to call it to the attention of the media. Stories of peace and harmony are simply not going to be reported to the same extent as violent confrontation. Nonetheless, these stories will eventually find their way into the public's eye and serve as an example for others.

Besides communicating a feeling of unity to the media, we must also exhibit solidarity with each other. When a minority person is placed in a position of responsibility, we should make every effort to support that person, unless he or she is either incompetent or unwilling to perform the requirements of the position. We must not expect these people, whether they be civic, political, religious, or business leaders, to pander to us. We can thwart any divide and conquer strategy by refusing to be divided.

When problems do emerge between our communities, rather than rushing to the media or to cynical Whites, we should first talk to each other. We should start with the assumption that we can work out our own problems and difficulties. If we cannot resolve disagreements by direct communication with each other, we can enlist the help of mediators to facilitate the communication. The process can be as simple as selecting a respected local individual in whom both sides have confidence to sit and listen in an attempt to resolve difficulties. Mediation of racial disputes works. It has worked to reduce tensions in schools and in neighborhoods. It worked for me when I mediated a 1995 dispute where an Amarillo, Texas, judge threatened a Hispanic woman with removal of her five-year-old daughter after the woman's ex-husband alleged that the mother was abusing the child by speaking Spanish to her. We can use existing dispute resolution systems where they exist and where they involve fair-minded people of all races who are interested in working toward peace and justice for the Black and Latino communities.

10. Emulate Those Seeking to Mend the Rifts between Blacks and Jews

Most of my suggestions for resolving conflict between Blacks and Hispanics require dialogue between those groups as the beginning of cooperation between them. To rebut those who might suggest that it is too simplistic to believe that conflict might begin to disappear through communication, I would cite the incredible peacemaking efforts between Jews and Blacks. Those efforts, seeking to reaffirm the historical cooperation between Jews and Blacks, revolve around dialogue.

A host of differences now plague both of these communities. Blacks felt resentment in 1978 when Jews called for the firing of Andrew Young from his position as United States Ambassador to the United Nations, after it became known that Young had conducted unauthorized meetings with the PLO. A year later Black and Jewish leaders publicly fought each other as some Jews took leadership roles in the anti-busing movement. A few years later, Louis Farrakhan made disparaging remarks about Judaism, and Jesse Jackson referred to New York City as "Hymietown." In 1991 Yankel Rosenbaum was murdered in the Crown Heights section of Brooklyn, with resulting disturbances involving Blacks and Jews. Other recent incidents, including the controversy surrounding the O. J. Simpson trial and disagreements over affirmative action, have led many Black and Jewish leaders to question whether their traditional alliance has broken apart.

That alliance, described by Cornel West as a major pillar of American progressive politics in this century, led to many of the civil rights gains won during the 1950s and 1960s. Jews made up more than half of the White Freedom Riders. Of the three martyrs of the Mississippi Summer, two were Jews and one was Black. The lobbying coalition that helped guide civil rights legislation through Congress was chaired by Clarence Mitchell of the NAACP and directed by Arnold Aronson of the National Jewish Community Relations Advisory Council. Other instances of Black-Jewish cooperation would require a volume to detail, but the efforts produced the hard-fought gains, such as implementing the Black right to vote which many now take for granted.

Yet this cooperation was not automatic. Tension existed between early Jewish immigrants and American Blacks. Cornel West attributes the beginning of a Black/Jewish alliance to the supportive links created by W. E. B. Du Bois's *The Crisis,* and Abraham Cahan's *Jewish Daily Forward,* and other writings and organizational contacts between Blacks and Jews beginning around 1910. These first, and ultimately successful, steps revolved around communication and dialogue. Now, as the alliance appears to weaken, communication again is the key. In numerous academic, literary, and political circles, calls are being made for dialogue. One of the most notable involves the decision in 1996 by Howard University and the American Jewish Committee to publish *CommonQuest,* a magazine that seeks to provide a forum for discussion of Black-Jewish relations in an atmosphere it describes as "beyond frenzy and accusation." A review of academic and popular publications reveals an explosion in the number of articles calling for enhanced communication between the two groups. In St. Louis, an African-American Jewish Dialogue Committee has been meeting monthly for the past five years, and the National Jewish Community Relations Advisory Council reports improving Black-Jewish relations in communities where coalitions have been established.

It takes courage to call for a discussion of these Black/Jewish disagreements, and even more courage to participate in the discussion. Extremists on both sides of the issue denounce each other. Even the more moderate voices within each group find themselves subject to public criticism by more aggressive members of their own group. Yet the dialogue continues, and in the process a renewed Black/Jewish alliance may be emerging. Certainly relations between the groups are improving, even where fundamental political differences, such as affirmative action, remain.

Similarly, Blacks and Latinos need to emulate the scholars and leaders who have begun the Black/Jewish peacemaking efforts. In some regards we are seventy years behind them, because we have not yet built a Black/Hispanic alliance in the first instance. Black and Latino scholars should emulate a process begun by DuBois and Cahan, by Elliot Cohen and James Baldwin, and others. It may be premature to begin publication of a Black/Brown *CommonQuest*, but that date is not far off. We need scholars like Henry Louis Gates, Jr., who courageously condemns anti-Semitism among some Blacks, to offer comparable testimonials regarding anti-Black sentiments among some Hispanics, and vice versa. We need political leaders to join in this call and in this process. And we need our community leaders and organizations to begin to talk to one another in an attempt to create Black, Jewish, and Latino coalitions.

11. Work for the Betterment of All America

Those of us who were born in this country are very fortunate indeed. Despite all of its troubles and difficulties, this country offers the greatest hope for economic advancement and the recognition of human rights in the world. This reality is the magnet that is drawing people from around the world to our shores and our borders.

Living in this blessed land carries with it the obligation to cherish it and to protect it. It behooves us as minorities to resist the temptation to work for narrow self-interest and short-term gratification in a struggle with other minority groups. Just as White Americans have an obligation to treat minorities fairly, so too do minority Americans have an obligation to work for the betterment of a society in which Whites will benefit. After all, a rising tide will lift all boats. We must reject the views of those who are shortsighted and cynical, and we must constantly endeavor to make this an even better country for our children. This is our country. We really have no other option. As Darrin Read, a student at Le Hair Barber College in Pleasant Grove, Texas, observed, "We are here together. They can't go back to Mexico and we can't go back to Africa."[3]

Notes

NOTES TO CHAPTER 1

1. David Treadwell, "Dixie's Hidden Minority: Anti-Latino Biases Rise in Old South," *Los Angeles Times*, July 11, 1987, at 1.
2. 118 CONG. REC. S 26664 (1972) (statement of Sen. Montoya).
3. Howard Kurtz, "Hughes Remarks Anger Hispanics," *Washington Post*, Feb. 22, 1994, at D01.
4. Roger E. Hernandez, "Tensions Split Hispanics, Blacks," *Rocky Mountain News*, Aug. 9, 1991, at 68.
5. Karen Bates, "Perspectives on Race Relations: Don't Muzzle the Messenger," *Los Angeles Times*, July 18, 1993, Op. sec., at 5.

NOTES TO CHAPTER 2

1. "Foreigners in Their Native Land: Historical Roots of the Mexican Americans" 33 (David J. Weber ed., 1973), cited in Juan Perea, "Los Olvidados: On the Making of Invisible People," 70 N.Y.U. L. Rev. 965, n. 52 (1995).
2. David Stannard, *American Holocaust* (1992), cited in Bill Piatt, *Immigration Law Cases and Materials* (1994), at 8.
3. W. Beck, *New Mexico: A History of Four Centuries* (1962), at 231.

4. Benjamin Franklin, "Observations Concerning the Increase of Mankind, Peopling of Countries, etc." (1751), cited in Perea, supra note 1, at n. 34.

5. Mark Reisler, *By the Sweat of Their Brow* (1976), at 152.

NOTES TO CHAPTER 3

1. Roger E. Hernandez, "Hispanic Unity Still Only a Hope," *Rocky Mountain News*, Aug. 12, 1994, Editorial, at 51A.

2. *Budinsky v. Corning Glass Works*, 425 F.Supp. 786, 788 (W.D. Pa. 1977).

3. *Manzanares v. Safeway Stores, Inc.*, 593 F.2d 968, 971 (1979).

4. Pat Shipman, "Facing Racial Differences—Together," *Chronicle of Higher Education*, Aug. 3, 1994, at B1.

5. Deborah Ramirez, "Multicultural Empowerment: It's Not Just Black and White Anymore," 47 Stan. L. Rev. 957 (1995), n. 47.

NOTES TO CHAPTER 4

1. Boisjoly, Greg J. Duncan, "Job Losses Among Hispanics in the Recent Recession," U.S. Dept. of Labor, *Monthly Labor Review,* June 1994, at 16.

2. Reginald Leamon Robinson, "The Other against Itself: Deconstructing the Violent Discourse between Korean and African Americans," 67 S.Cal. L. Rev. 15, p. 76 and related notes (1993).

3. Douglas S. Massey and Nancy A. Denton, "*American Apartheid: Segregation and the Making of the Underclass*" (1993).

4. Stephanie Chavez, "Racial Tensions over South L.A. Jobs Grow," *Los Angeles Times,* July 22, 1992, Metro sec., at 1.

NOTES TO CHAPTER 5

1. Frederick Douglass, *Narrative of the Life of Frederick Douglass, an American Slave* (1960), at 65 (first pub. 1845).

2. *Brown v. Board of Education of Topeka*, 347 U.S. 483, 495 (1954).

3. James S. Kunen, "The End of Integration," *Time*, April 29, 1996, at 44.

NOTES TO CHAPTER 6

1. Jonetta Rose Barras and Vincent McGraw, "Moving Up and Moving In," *Washington Times*, May 9, 1993, at A1.

2. See Bill Piatt, "*¿Only English? Law and Language Policy in the United States*" (1990), at 174–76.

3. Transcript of Proceedings, Hearing on Motion to Modify "In the Interest of Faviola Areli Garcia, a Minor Child," 181st District Court, Randall County, Texas, no. 33,733–B, June 30, 1995, at 32.

4. Larry Rohter, "As Hispanic Presence Grows, So Does Black Anger," *New York Times*, June 20, 1993, at 1.

5. W. E. B. Du Bois, "French and Spanish," April 1919, from "The Emerging Thought of W. E. B. Du Bois" (Henry Lee Moon ed., 1972), at 127.

NOTES TO CHAPTER 7

1. Seth Mydans, "Desert Playground for Rich Is Turf for Racial Gang War," *New York Times*, March 18, 1994, at A16.

2. Rosalind Muhammad, "Black-Latino Gangs Offer Peace to L.A. Neighborhood," *Final Call*, Aug. 30, 1995, at 7.

3. Mike Davis, "In L.A., Burning All Illusions: Urban America Sees Its Future," *Nation*, June 1, 1992, at 743.

NOTES TO CHAPTER 8

1. *Louisiana v. United States*, 380 U.S. 145, 153 (1965).

2. For those readers interested in the math, the following formula determines the number of votes needed to elect officials under cumulative voting:

$$\frac{nV}{O + 1} + 1$$

n represents the number of officials one wishes to elect, V equals the total number of voters, O equals the number of officials to be elected. Since this book is not a math primer, I will not set out some of the calculations. The bottom line is that minority voters could cumulate their votes and guarantee election of minority representatives.

NOTES TO CHAPTER 9

1. Charles R. Lawrence, III, "Forward Ace, Multiculturalism, and the Jurisprudence of Transformation," 47 Stan. L. Rev. 819, 829 (1995).

2. "The Talented Tenth: Memorial Address," In *W. E. B. Du Bois: A Reader* (David Lewis ed., 1995), at 347–53.

3. Catalina Camia et al., "Fusion and Friction," *Dallas Morning News,* Oct. 18, 1992, at 1A.

Bibliography

BOOKS

W. Beck, "New Mexico: A History of Four Centuries" (1962).

Frederick Douglass, "Narrative of the Life of Frederick Douglass, an American Slave" (1960) (first pub. 1845).

"W. E. B. DuBois: A Reader" (David Levering Lewis ed., 1995).

"The Emerging Thought of W. E. B. DuBois" (Henry Lee Moon ed., 1972).

Ernest Gruening, "Mexico and Its Heritage" (1934).

Lani Guinier, "The Tyranny of the Majority: Fundamental Fairness in Representative Democracy" (1994).

Douglas S. Massey and Nancy A. Denton, "American Apartheid: Segregation and the Making of the Underclass" (1993).

Kenneth Meier and Joseph Stewart, Jr., "Politics of Hispanic Education: Un Paso Pa'lante Y Dos Pa'tras" (1991).

Leon C. Metz, "Border: The U.S.–Mexico Line" (1989).

Fernando Orozco, "Historia de Mexico" (1982).

Colin A. Palmer, "Slaves of the White God: Blacks in Mexico, 1570–1650" (1976).

Bill Piatt, "Immigration Law: Cases and Materials" (1994).

Bill Piatt, "Language on the Job: Balancing Business Needs and Employee Rights" (1993).

Bill Piatt, "¿Only English? Law and Language Policy in the United States" (1990).

Mark Reisler, "By the Sweat of Their Brow" (1976).

185

David Stannard, "American Holocaust" (1992).
Hanni U. Taylor, "Standard English, Black English, and Bidialectalism" (1989).
Cornel West, "Race Matters" (1993).
Stephanie M. Wildman, "Privilege Revealed: How Invisible Preference Undermines America" (1996).

ARTICLES

Catherine Abrams, "Raising Politics Up: Minority Political Participation and Section 2 of the Voting Rights Act," 63 N.Y.U. L. Rev. 449 (1988).
Frank Adams, Jr., "Why Brown v. Board of Education and Affirmative Action Can Save Historically Black Colleges and Universities," 47 Ala. L. Rev. 481 (1996).
Angelo N. Ancheta and Katheryn K. Imahara, "Multi-Ethnic Voting Rights: Redefining Vote Dilution in Communities of Color," 27 U.S.F. L. Rev. 815 (1993).
Lorrin Anderson, "Crime, Race and the Fourth Estate," National Review, Oct. 15, 1990, at 52.
Jonetta Rose Barras and Vincent McGraw, "Moving Up and Moving In," Washington Times, May 9, 1993, at A1.
Karen Bates, "Perspectives on Race Relations: Don't Muzzle the Messenger," Los Angeles Times, July 18, 1993, Op. sec., at 5.
Joanne Boisjoly and Greg J. Duncan, "Job Losses among Hispanics in the Recent Recession," U.S. Dept. of Labor Monthly Labor Review, June 1994, at 16.
John O. Calmore, "Racialized Space and the Culture of Segregation: 'Hewing a Stone of Hope from a Mountain of Despair,' " 143 U. Pa. L. Rev. 1233 (1995).
Catalina Camia et al., "Fusion and Friction," Dallas Morning News, Oct. 18, 1992, at 1A.
Robert S. Capers, "Census Finds Gains, Disparities for Blacks," Hartford Courant, Feb. 23, 1995, at A1.
Peter Cattan, "The Diversity of Hispanics in the U.S. Workforce," U.S. Dept. of Labor Monthly Labor Review, Aug. 1993, at 3.
Stephanie Chavez, "Racial Tensions over South L.A. Jobs Grow," Los Angeles Times, July 22, 1992, Metro sec., at 1.
Alice H. Choi, "A Closer Look at the Conflict between the African-American and the Korean-American Communities in

South Central Los Angeles," 1 Asian Am. Pac. Is. L. J. 69 (1993).

Richard E. Cohen, "Changing the Rules of Redistricting," National Journal, June 22, 1996, at 1383.

Colloquy, "Our Next Race Question: The Uneasiness between Blacks and Latinos," Harper's Magazine, April 1996, at 55.

"Dadz in the 'Hood: Gang Warfare," The Economist, Nov. 4, 1995, at 33.

Mike Davis, "In L.A., Burning All Illusions: Urban America Sees Its Future," The Nation, June 1, 1992, at 743.

Gabriel Escobar, "Treatment of D.C. Latinos Called 'Appalling' by Panel," Washington Post, Feb. 6, 1993, at A01.

Darryl Fears, "Analysis: Population Shifts Strain Unity among Minorities," Atlanta Constitution, July 24, 1994, at F1.

Andres Ford, "Blacks, Jews Take New Steps to Heal Divisions," Los Angeles Times, June 10, 1996, at B1.

Malcolm Gladwell, "Black Like Them," New Yorker, April 29 and May 6, 1996, at 74.

"Grady Timeline," Santa Fe New Mexican, Feb. 9, 1996, at A4.

Bernard Grofman, "Voting Rights in a Multi-Ethnic World," 13 Chicano-Latino L. Rev. 15 (1993).

Lani Guinier, "The Representation of Minority Interests: The Question of Single-Member Districts," 14 Cardozo L. Rev. 1135 (1993).

Lani Guinier, "The Triumph of Tokenism: The Voting Rights Act and the Theory of Black Electoral Success," 89 Mich. L. Rev. 1077 (1991).

Jay Hancock, "State Ranks Second in Black-Run Firms; U.S. Cites Area's Core of Middle Class African-Americans," Baltimore Sun, Dec. 12, 1995, at 1C.

Jacquelyn Heard, "Racial Strife Runs Deep at High School: Black and Hispanic Staff, Students Clash at Farragut," Chicago Tribune, Nov. 17, 1992, at 1.

Roger E. Hernandez, "Hispanic Unity Still Only a Hope," Rocky Mountain News, Aug. 12, 1994, Editorial, at 51A.

Roger E. Hernandez, "Tensions Split Hispanics, Blacks," Rocky Mountain News, Aug. 9, 1991, at 68.

Jonathan P. Hicks, "Trying to Find a Common Ground," New York Times, March 10, 1996, sec. 1, at 35.

Lucy Hood, "Hispanic-Owned Businesses Multiplying Fast," Lubbock Avalanche Journal, July 3, 1996, at 7C.

Chet W. Hye, "Supreme Court Draws a Line in the Sand—The Color Line," Denver Post, June 20, 1996, at B7.

Jesse Katz, "Clashes between Latino, Black Gangs Increase," Los Angeles Times, Dec. 26, 1993, at A1.

James S. Kunen, "The End of Integration," Time Magazine, April 29, 1996, at 39.

Howard Kurtz, "Hughes Remarks Anger Hispanics," Washington Post, Feb. 22, 1994, at D01.

David Lamb, "Home on the Range—Where Blacks Are Finding a Haven," Los Angeles Times, April 8, 1993, at A3.

Charles R. Lawrence, III, "Forward Ace, Multiculturalism, and the Jurisprudence of Transformation," 47 Stan. L. Rev. 819 (1995).

John H. Lee, "Bullets and Immigrants Struggle," Los Angeles Times, April 7, 1992, at B3.

Fred W. Lindecke, "Black and Jewish Leaders Think Positive," St. Louis Post-Dispatch, Oct. 18, 1995, at 5B.

James Loewen, "Levels of Political Mobilization and Racial Bloc Voting among Latinos, Anglos, and African-Americans in New York City," 13 Chicano-Latino L. Rev. 38 (1993).

Nora Lopez, "Leaders' Meeting Adds to Discord among Trustees," Dallas Morning News, May 21, 1996, at 13A.

Audrey Steinbergen Lundy, "Racial Cooperation Advocated: Blacks, Hispanics Urged to Join Forces to Solve Mutual Problems," Dallas Morning News, April 9, 1996, at 1Y.

Anna Macias, "Parents and Officials Discuss Pinkston High Racial Tension," Dallas Morning News, March 23, 1993, at 20A.

George A. Martinez, "Legal Indeterminacy: Judicial Discretion and the Mexican-American Litigation Experience 1930–1980," 27 U.C. Davis L. Rev. 555 (1994).

Allen McConagha, "Rift between Blacks, Hispanics Tears Up Movement from Within," Washington Times, May 28, 1991, at A1.

Antonio McDaniel, "The Dynamic Racial Composition of the United States: An American Dilemma Revisited," Daedalus, American Academy of Arts and Sciences, Jan. 1995, at 179.

Cord Meyer, "Forthcoming Transformation of Texas?" Washington Times, May 26, 1995, at A21.

Jack Miles, "Blacks v. Browns: African-Americans and Latinos," The Atlantic, Oct. 1992, at 41.

Rosalind Muhammad, "Black-Latino Gangs Offer Peace to LA Neighborhood," The Final Call, Aug. 30, 1995, at 7.

Seth Mydans, "Desert Playground for Rich Is Turf for Racial Gang War," New York Times, March 18, 1994, at A16.

Seth Mydans, "Racial Tensions in Los Angeles Jails Ignite Inmate Violence," New York Times, Feb. 6, 1995, at A13.

Ben Neary, "Both Sides Say There Are Five Votes against Grady," Santa Fe New Mexican, Aug. 16, 1995, at A1.

Ben Neary, "Council May Change Law to Fire Chief," Santa Fe New Mexican, Aug. 18, 1995, at A1.

Ben Neary, "Pino: I Won't Fire the Chief," Santa Fe New Mexican, Aug. 17, 1995, at A1.

Angela E. Oh, "Race Relations in Los Angeles: 'Divide and Conquer' Is Alive and Flourishing," 66 S. Cal. L. Rev. 1647 (1993).

Laura Parker, "Violence after Police Shooting Exposes Miami Racial Tension," Washington Post, June 29, 1991, at A2.

Juan Perea, "Los Olvidados: On the Making of Invisible People," 70 N.Y.U. L. Rev. 965 (1995).

Deborah Ramirez, "Multi-Cultural Empowerment: It's Not Just Black and White Anymore," 47 Stan. L. Rev. 957 (1995).

William Raspberry, "Race Conscious Race," Washington Post, March 18, 1983, at A19.

Patty Reinert, "Amarillo Judge Does About-Face," Houston Chronicle, Sept. 19, 1995, at A11.

Lisa Richardson, "Teaching Tolerance: High Schools Implement Programs to Help Ease Racial Tensions," Los Angeles Times, May 12, 1994, at J11.

Larry Rohter, "As Hispanic Presence Grows, So Does Black Anger," New York Times, June 20, 1993, at 1.

Carlos Sanchez, "Redirecting Racial Tensions: Blacks, Hispanics Ask Dixon for Study," Washington Post, June 28, 1991, Metro sec., at B3.

Alex M. Saragoza et al., "History and Public Policy, Title VII and the Use of the Hispanic Classification," 5 La Raza L. J. 1 (1992).

William E. Schmidt, "Denver Election Widens Circle of Hispanic Leaders," New York Times, June 23, 1983, at A16.

Pat Shipman, "Facing Racial Differences—Together," Chronicle of Higher Education, Aug. 3, 1994, at B1.

Peter Skerry, "E Pluribus Hispanic?" Wilson Quarterly, Summer 1992, at 62.

Rennard Strickland, "Strangers in a Strange Land: A Historical Perspective of the Columbian Quincentenary," 7 St. John's J. Legal Comment, 571 (1992).

Steve Terrell, "Blacks Allege Racism, Plan Friday Rally," Santa Fe New Mexican, Aug. 16, 1995, at A1.

David Treadwell, "Dixie's Hidden Minority: Anti-Latino Biases Rise in Old South," Los Angeles Times, July 11, 1987, at 1.

Ann Scott Tyson, "Ethnic, Economic Divisions of U.S. Growing," Christian Science Monitor, July 7, 1994, at 3.

Georges Vernez, David Ronfeldt, "The Current Situation in Mexican Immigration," Science, American Association for the Advancement of Science, March 8, 1991, at 1189.

Jill Walker, "Surge of Hispanic Gangs Seen in Los Angeles, Move into Traditionally Black Areas Reported," Washington Post, May 29, 1990, at A3.

Kathy Walt, "Inmates to Get Training in 'Cultural Sensitivity,'" Houston Chronicle, May 19, 1996, State sec., at 1.

Henry Weinstein, "Tensions Escalate between Leaders of Blacks, Latinos," Los Angeles Times, July 11, 1992, at A1.

Roger Wilson, "Repairing Race Relations: Racial Problems in the U.S.," Spectrum: The Journal of State Government, June 22, 1993, at 8.

Lawrence Wright, "One Drop of Blood," New Yorker, July 25, 1994, at 46.

COURT CASES

Brown v. Board of Education of Topeka, 347 U.S. 483 (1954).

Budinsky v. Corning Glass Works, 425 F. Supp. 786 (W.D.Pa. 1977).

Bush et al. v. Vera et al., 116 S.Ct. 1941 (1996).

Garcia v. Spun Steak Co., 998 F.2d 1480 (9th Cir. 1993), cert. denied 114 S.Ct. 2726 (1994).

Hernandez v. Driscoll Consolidated Independent School District, 2 Race Rel. L. Rptr. 329 (S.D. Tex. 1957).

Hopwood v. Texas, 84 F.3d 720 (5th Cir. 1996), cert. denied, 1996 WL227009 (1996).

Independent School District v. Salvatierra, 33 S.W.2d 790 (Tex. Civ. App. 1930), cert. denied, 284 U.S. 580 (1931).

In the Interest of Faviola Areli Garcia, a Minor Child, 181st District Court, Randall County, Texas, No. 33,733–B.

Louisiana v. United States, 380 U.S. 145 (1965).

Loving v. Virginia, 388 U.S. 1 (1967).

Manzanares v. Safeway Stores, Inc., 593 F.2d 968 (10th Cir. 1979).

Martin Luther King, Jr., Elementary School Children v. Ann Arbor School District Board, 473 F. Supp. 1371 (E.D.Mich. 1979).

Milliken v. Bradley, 418 U.S. 717 (1974).

Plessy v. Ferguson, 163 U.S. 537 (1896).

Podberesky v. Kirwan, 38 F.3d 147 (4th Cir. 1994), cert. denied, 115 S.Ct. 2001 (1995).

Regents of the University of California v. Bakke, 438 U.S. 265 (1978).

U.S. v. Fordice, 505 U.S. 717 (1992).

U.S. v. Texas, 342 F.Supp. 24 (E.D.Tex. 1971).

Westminster School District v. Mendez, 161 F.2d 774 (9th Cir. 1947).

OTHER SOURCES

Bureau of the Census, U.S. Dep't. of Commerce, 1990 Census of Population, General Population Characteristics (1991).

"Demographically Speaking: African-American Population Profile," Minority Markets Alert, Dec. 1993, p. 178.

"Demographics Are Changing in America's Big Cities," National Public Radio Morning Edition, Jan. 31, 1996, transcript no. 1793–14.

L. H. Research, Lou Harris, Study Director, "Taking America's Pulse: The Full Report of the National Conference Survey on Intergroup Relations," study no. 930019, 1994.

National Council of La Raza, Poverty Project Fact Sheet, Jan. 1996.

National Hispanic Leadership Agenda, "1996 Policy Summary," May 1996.

Standards for the Classification of Federal Data on Race and Ethnicity, Advance Notice of Proposed Review and Possible Revision of OMB's Statistical Policy Directive No. 15, 59 Fed. Reg. 29,831, 29,832 (1994).

"Supreme Court Rules against Minority Voting Districts," National Public Radio Morning Edition, June 14, 1996, transcript no. 1890–1.

The United States Census Bureau, "The Black Population in the United States: March 1994 and 1993" (P.20–480).

United States Census Bureau: "Characteristics of the Black Population: 1990 (CP-3–6).

FOR FURTHER READING

Derrick Bell, "And We Are Not Saved: The Elusive Quest for Racial Justice" (1987).

Derrick Bell, "Faces at the Bottom of the Well" (1992).

"Black Language Reader" (Robert H. Bentley and Samuel D. Crawford, eds., 1973).

Robert Edgar Conrad, "Children of God's Fire: A Documentary History of Black Slavery in Brazil" (1983).

"Perspectives on Black English" (J. Dillard, ed., 1975).

George M. Frederickson, "The Black in the White Mind: The Debate on Afro-American Character and Destiny, 1817–1914" (1972).

Andrew Hacker, "Two Nations" (1992).

Christine Hunefeldt, "Paying the Price of Freedom: Family and Labor among Lima's Slaves" (1994).

James H. Johnson and Walter C. Farrel, Jr., "The Fire This Time: The Genesis of the Los Angeles Rebellion of 1992," 71 N.C. L. Rev. 1403 (1993).

John V. Lombardi, "The Decline and Abolition of Negro Slavery in Venezuela 1820–1854" (1971).

"Form and Function in Chicano English" (Jacob Ornstein-Galicia, ed., 1984).

William Frederick Sharp, "Slavery on the Spanish Frontier" (1976).

George Sinkler, "The Racial Attitudes of American Presidents: From Abraham Lincoln to Theodore Roosevelt" (1971).

Hanni U. Taylor, "Standard English, Black English and Bidialectalism" (1989).

Robert D. Twiggs, "Pan African Language in the Western Hemisphere" (1973).

Index

accents, 99–104
Africa, 13, 20, 167, 179
African-American Jewish Dialogue
    Committee, 177
African Americans
    See Blacks
Africans, 14, 15, 16, 17, 18, 20, 24, 25,
    27, 159
Alamo, 19
Ali, Muhammad, 10
Allport, Gordon, 59
Amarillo, Texas, 175
Amaya, Joaquin, 102
American Jewish Committee, 177
Anglos, 9, 43
    See also Caucasians; Whites
Arizona, 15
Aronson, Arnold, 177
Asia, 13
Asian Americans
    demographic comparisons, 1, 2
    gangs, 121
    mixed marriages, 43, 44
    voting, 132, 142

assimilation, 26–27, 42
Atwater, Lee, 137

Badillo, Herman, 141
Baldwin, James, 178
Bilingual Education Act of 1968,
    78
Black English, 99, 103–104
Blacks
    businesses, 166–168
    coalitions with Hispanics, 141–145,
        147–149, 153–179
    definitional issues, 38–48, 159
    demographic comparisons, 1, 2,
        30, 48, 54–56, 58–59, 114, 166
    educational issues, 67–90
    employment issues, 49–66
    gangs, 109–123
    immigration, 13–23
    language issues, 91–108
    mixed marriages, 16–17, 22, 43–
        48
    overview of relations with Hispan-
        ics, 4–12

Blacks *(Continued)*
  relations with Jews, 175–178
  voting, 124–152
  See also African Americans
Box, John C., 22
Bradley, Tom, 7, 146
Brazil, 17
Breyer, Stephen, 33
Brooke, Ed, 146
Brown
  See Hispanics
Brown, Ron, 167
Brown, Willie, 146
Brown v. Board of Education of Topeka, 69, 70, 75, 77
Bush, George, 158
Bush, George W., 136
Bush, Jeb, 158

Cabranes, Jose, 33
Cahan, Abraham, 177, 178
Canada, 14
Caraballo, Wilfredo, 33
Caribbean, 24, 38, 157–158, 167
caste system, 16–17
Catholic, 15, 29, 30
Caucasians, 15
  See also Anglos; Whites
census
  See United States Census Bureau
Chavez, Cesar, 10
Chicago, 8, 115, 120, 124, 126–127, 143
Chicano, 30
  See also Mexican Americans
Chinese Americans, 170
Civil Rights Act of 1866, 34
Civil Rights Act of 1957, 129
Civil Rights Act of 1964, 27–28, 30, 41, 79, 129
Clinton, William, 33, 152
coalitions, 141–145, 147–149, 153–179
Cohen, Elliot, 178

Colorado, 15, 135
Columbus, Christopher, 14
CommonQuest, 177
Community Build, 123
Cortez, Hernan, 14
Cuba, 14
Cuban Americans
  definitional issues, 30–31, 32–33
  demographic comparisons, 48
  tension with Blacks in Miami, 5–6
  voting, 140
cumulative voting, 150–152

Daley, Richard M., 143
Dallas, Texas, 10, 115, 124, 135, 143–144
Davis, Mike, 122
de Alva, Jorge Klor, 45
Del Rio, Texas, 76
demographic comparisons, 1–3, 30, 48, 54–57, 58–59, 114
Denver, Colorado, 126, 146
Dinkins, David, 142, 145, 148
Douglass, Frederick, 68, 81
DuBois, W. E. B., 105–106, 163, 177, 178

education, 67–90
  affirmative action, 82–87
  bilingual education, 78–80
  scholarships, 84, 87–89
  segregation, 68–81
Ehrlich, Everet, 166
employment, 49–66
English language, 11, 17, 19, 26, 27, 53
  See also language issues; voting, literacy tests
Equal Educational Opportunity Act, 79
equal protection, 69–71
  See also Fourteenth Amendment
Europe, 14
Europeans, 16, 17, 21, 25–27, 31

Farrakhan, Louis, 176
Farrell, Herman D., 141
Ferrer, Fernando, 142, 143
Fifteenth Amendment, 127, 130, 133
First Amendment, 173
Florida, 14, 33, 139, 140
Forester, Robert, 21
Forman, Michael, 100
Fourteenth Amendment, 69–71, 133, 136
Fragrante, Manuel T., 99–100
Franklin, Benjamin, 20
Franks, Gary, 146

gangs, 109–123
Garcia v. Spun Steak Co., 53
Gates, Henry Louis, Jr., 178
Georgia, 138
Gingrich, Newt, 138
Giuliani, Rudolph W., 142
Glass Ceiling Commission, 58
Grady, Donald, 49–51
Grant, Madison, 21

Hailius, Latasha, 122
Haitians, 32, 38
Harris, Louis, 9, 57, 154, 164
Hart, Albert, 21
Hayward, Melvin, 119
Hernandez v. Driscoll Consolidated Independent School District, 77–78
Hopwood v. Texas, 83–84
Hidalgo, Miguel, 161
Hispanics
   businesses, 166–168
   coalitions with Blacks, 141–145, 147–149, 153–179
   definitional issues, 29–48, 159
   demographic comparisons, 1–2, 30, 48, 54–56, 58–59, 114, 166
   educational issues, 67–90
   gangs, 109–123
   immigration, 13–23
   language issues, 91–108
   mixed marriages, 16–17, 22, 43–48
   overview of relations with Blacks, 4–12
   voting, 124–152
historically Black colleges and universities, 73–75
Honolulu, Hawaii, 99
Houston, Texas, 23, 124, 144
Hughes, Kathy, 8

immigration, 13–23
Immigration Reform and Control Act, 56
Indians, 16, 17, 18, 21, 22, 34
   See also Native Americans
Italian Americans, 139

Jackson, Jesse, 145, 176
Jamaicans, 38–39
Jaramillo, Debbie, 51
Jefferson, Thomas, 20, 171
Jenkins, Thomas A., 22
Jews, 175–178
jobs, 49–66
Johnson, Lyndon, 130

Kansas City, Missouri, 70–71, 119
Katzenbach v. Morgan, 131–132
Kelly, Sharon, 8
Kerner Commission, 28
King, Rodney, 11
Koch, Ed, 141, 142
Korean Americans, 39, 121–122, 156, 167, 168
Ku Klux Klan, 51

language issues, 91–108
   voting, 128–134
Laredo, Texas, 101
Latinos
   See Hispanics
Laughlin, Harry, 22

Laureano, Marta, 97–98
Law School Admission Test, 84–85
League of United Latin American Citizens, 31
literacy tests
See voting
Los Angeles, 7, 9, 10, 11, 23, 111, 112, 114, 116, 118, 119, 121, 122, 124, 126, 127, 146, 167, 174
Louisiana, 83, 129
Loving v. Virginia, 41
Lozano, William, 6
Lubbock, Texas, 9

Mandela, Nelson, 6
Massachusetts, 20
McCall, H. Carl, 143
Mejia v. New York, 99–100
Metro Broadcasting, Inc. v. FCC, 45
Mexican Americans
celebration of 16th of September, 160–161
definitional issues, 30–35
demographic comparisons, 48
deportation, 22
Mexican Mafia, 114
Mexicans, 4, 15, 19, 21, 22
Mexico, 14, 18, 19, 20, 33, 157
Miami, Florida, 5, 6, 33, 106, 161
Milliken v. Bradley, 70
Minneapolis, Minnesota, 120
Mississippi, 9, 83
Missouri v. Jenkins, 71
Mitchell, Clarence, 177
mixed race background, 16–17, 22, 43–48
See also multicultural; multiracial
Monroe, James, 20
Montoya, Joseph M., 5
Moors, 15–16
Moseley-Braun, Carol, 146
Moynihan, Daniel Patrick, 56

multicultural, 2–3
See also mixed race background; multiracial
Multicultural Collaborative, 118
multiracial, 2, 45–48, 122
See also mixed race background; multicultural
Multiracial Americans of Southern California, 122
Muslims, 15–16

NAACP, 51, 56, 177
National Jewish Community Relations Advisory Council, 177, 178
national origin discrimination, 34–37
Native Americans
America stolen from, 170
demographic comparisons, 1–2
destruction of, 17–18
immigration, 13
mixed marriages, 16–18, 22, 43–44
voting, 132
"What are they like?" 75–76
Negroes
See Blacks
New Mexico, 15, 19, 20, 28, 78, 157
Newton, Steve, Jr., 115
New York, 131–132, 143
New York City, 8, 10, 23, 39, 121, 124, 126, 141–143, 161, 174
North Carolina, 128, 137, 149

O'Connor, Sandra, 136
official-English, 96–98
Oklahoma, 128, 146
Olmos, Eddie, 112
Onate, Juan de, 15
"one drop" rule, 40, 41
Orozco, Fernando, 19

Peabody, Endicott, 146
Peña, Federico, 146
Phoenix, Arizona, 23
Pleasant Grove, Texas, 179

Plessy v. Ferguson, 40–41, 69, 77
Podberesky v. Kirwan, 87–89
Polk, James, 18
Ponce de Leon, Juan, 14
Powell, Colin, 146
Powell, Lewis, 82, 83
Puerto Ricans
    definitional issues, 30–31, 32–37
    demographic comparison, 48
    voting, 131

race
    conflicts used as control, 52–53
    definitional problems, 29–48
    perception, 45, 159
    self-identification, 37, 41–48, 159
racial discrimination, 34–36, 168
    *See also under specific minority
        groups*
Rangel, Charles B., 142
Read, Davin, 179
*Regents of the University of California
    v. Bakke,* 82–83
Reynoso, Cruz, 162
Rosenbaum, Yankel, 176
Roybal, Edward, 36
Roybal, Pete, 28

St. Louis, Missouri, 177
Saltonstall, Leverett, 146
San Antonio, Texas, 23, 124
San Francisco, California, 146
San Francisco Fire Department, 28–
    29
Santa Fe, New Mexico, 15, 49–51, 75,
    102
Serrano, José E., 142
Shakely, Jack, 9
Shorris, Earl, 45
Simpson, O. J., 176
slavery, 14, 18, 27, 28, 68, 81, 127–
    128, 171
Small Business Administration, 168
Smith, Susan, 61

Southwest Voter Registration Project,
    147
Spain, 15, 16, 29, 31
Spaniards, 14–17, 28–29, 157
Spanish language, 9, 11, 29, 30, 52–
    53
    See also language issues
Suarez, Xavier, 6
*Swann v. Charlotte-Mecklenburg Board
    of Education,* 69
Switzer, Barry, 170

Tacoma Park, Maryland, 127
Texas, 15, 18, 83–84, 89, 117, 122, 135,
    149, 160
Thomas, Clarence, 71
Tsongas, Paul, 146
Treaty of Guadalupe Hidalgo, 19

United States, 13, 14, 18, 19, 20, 21,
    22, 30, 32, 33, 34, 179
United States Census Bureau, 1, 2,
    22, 28, 31, 166
United States Department of Com-
    merce, 166, 167
United States Department of Health
    Education and Welfare, 78
United States Equal Employment
    Opportunity Commission, 37,
    64
United States Office of Management
    and Budget, 45
United States v. Fordyce, 73–74

Virginia, 18
voting, 124–152
    coalitions, 141–145, 147–149
    cumulative voting, 150–152
    districting, 134–140
    literacy tests, 128–134
    White vote, 145–147
    Who can vote? 126–134
Voting Rights Act of 1965, 130–134,
    136, 139, 140

Washington, D.C., 7, 10, 126, 144
Washington, George, 171
Washington, Harold, 143
Watkins, Brian, 121
Watts, J. C., 146
Weber, David, 15
West, Cornel, 45, 176
West Indians, 39
Whites
    defining who is Black or Brown,
        159
    definitional issues, 30–31, 34–36,
        40–48
    enlisting support of, 170–173

gangs, 109, 116
immigration, 25–27
nativism, 20–23
responsibility for Black/Hispanic
    conflict, 153–156
voting, 145–147, 148
White supremacy, 43, 81, 153–154,
    156
    See also Anglos; Caucasians
Wilder, Douglas, 146
Wildman, Stephanie, 172
Wisconsin, 20

Young, Andrew, 176